Retirement Planning

Copyright © 2022 Andrew J. Brown

All rights reserved. No part of this book may be reproduced, stored in a retrieval system, or transmitted in any form or by any means, electronic, mechanical, photocopying, recording, scanning, or otherwise, without the prior written permission of the author/publisher.

Table of Contents

Introduction _____ 6

Chapter 1: How To Get Ready for a Retirement Plan _____ 10

    Understanding What a Retirement Plan Is _____ 10

    Why do So Many Folks Not Plan for Retirement? 12

    The Stages of Retirement Planning _____ 13

    Vital Aspects of Retirement Planning _____ 15

    Retirement Planning Challenges_____ 16

    Preparing Comprehensively for Your Retirement Plan _____ 20

Chapter 2: How Much do You Need to Retire? _____ 26

    How Much Do You Need to Save for Retirement? 26

    Factors to Consider _____ 28

    The Bottom Line _____ 37

Chapter 3: Why Is Having a Retirement Plan Important? _____ 38

    Retirement Planning is VITAL _____ 39

    Bottom Line _____ 49

Chapter 4: How to Start Saving for Retirement _____ 50

Vital Tips on Saving Up for Retirement _____ 50

How to Start Saving for Retirement, Step by Step 53

Chapter 5: The Power of Compound Interest 60

What Is Compound Interest? _____ 60

Understanding Compound Interest Calculations_ 62

Pros and Cons of Compounding _____ 69

The Bottom Line _____ 72

Chapter 6: Accounts You Can Use to Invest In Retirement _____ 73

Key Plan Benefits to Consider _____ 73

The Best Retirement Plans to Consider In November 2022 And Beyond _____ 74

How Many Retirement Accounts Can I Have? __ 83

Chapter 7: How to Take Advantage of Social Security as Part of Your Retirement Plan __ 86

Before You Make a Decision to Withdraw Retirement Funds _____ 88

Strategies to Boost Your Benefits _____ 88

The Bottom Line _____ 95

Chapter 8: How to Invest for Retirement __ 96

Chapter 9: Streamline Your Retirement Income Sources _____ 106

Pointers to Build a Robust Investment Portfolio Asset Allocation _____ 106

Minimizing Portfolio Risks _____ 108

Working with a Financial Advisor to Further Streamline Your Portfolio _____ 109

Pros and Cons of Hiring a Financial Advisor ____ 110

Choosing a Financial Advisor: Key Questions to Ask _____ 111

Chapter 10: How To Proof Your Retirement Financially _____ 113

How To Pick Yourself Back Up In The Face of a Financial Setback _____ 117

Conclusion _____ 119

Retirement Planning Worksheets _____ 121

Introduction

We all want to live into our 90s and beyond; being able to grow old before we die is the ultimate blessing, after all. But with old age comes reduced vigor and diminished earning capacity. And most companies will retire you at 60 anyway and send you on your way.

So, what happens next?

Will you be adequately prepared, or will you be scrambling desperately, perennially weighed down by financially-induced worry?

If you are vigilant with saving up for retirement, you'll be set for the rest of your life. Unfortunately, too many of us do not take the prospect of retiring and not being able to bring in regular income anymore, all while being saddled with the same bills, with enough seriousness. And by doing so, we're setting ourselves up for a miserable time in our retirement years.

According to St. Louis (St. Louis Fed), the personal savings rate in America is at the lowest point since they started keeping track of the measurement in 1959. Therefore, it should not come as a huge surprise that a recent Harris Poll Research Consulting survey revealed that 34% of Americans have no retirement savings.

Another recent study discovered that only about 4 percent of people who start working at age 25 will have accumulated sufficient money for retirement by the time they reach age 65. In comparison, 63 percent will be totally dependent on Social Security, friends, family, or charity for survival.

Most Americans are either entirely unprepared for retirement or underprepared at best. We cannot place too much blame on the average American. We've been conditioned to spend, spend and spend.

No; Social Security Will Not Give You Security

Many people's current strategy is to spend what they make, save as little as possible, and rely on Social Security when they retire. But as many retirees, unfortunately, find out too late, Social Security was not designed to replace your income when you retire.

A lot of people misunderstand the concept of Social Security, what it truly means, and the 'extent of its powers.' This is why I feel we should start with understanding Social Security so that you'll be fully aware of whose hands you're trying to place your future in.

So, what is Social Security?

If you look carefully at your paycheck (and you should; it's crucial to study your paycheck and understand every single item on it), you'll probably notice a deduction that goes to OASDI. OASDI is an acronym for the Social Security Administration's Old-Age, Survivors, and Disability Insurance program.

Now, this is where a lot of people get it wrong. They think their Social Security deductions work like a 401(k) account where the deductions sit in an OASDI account with their names on it, waiting for them to cash it when they retire. But it doesn't work that way.

First, as absurd as this may sound, any Social Security deductions from your paycheck don't belong to you. The Social Security administration takes these deductions out of everyone's paychecks, pools everything together, and then uses it to pay the millions of Americans who currently qualify to receive Social Security payments.

So, no, your Social Security contributions are not contributions to your future pocket; they are the contributions you make to the government to better the lives of others – just like the taxes you pay so that you can live in a sane and developed society. So, the government takes this money to pay retirees, the disabled, children, and anyone who qualifies to receive Social Security.

So, what happens when you retire? Well, it's like karma - good karma.

You've been a good person your whole working life, contributing positively to the lives of others, and now, it's time for you to receive your rewards. Now, it's time for other people's contributions to fund your lifestyle.

But there's a clause.

First, don't expect to receive the exact money you contributed during your working years. Of course, the longer you've worked and contributed, the higher your Social Security checks will be in retirement. Still, conditions, criteria, and formulas are applied and used to calculate what will be due to you in Social Security checks when you retire. For example, your age is considered. Whatever age you decide to start claiming Social Security checks will affect the payout you'll receive.

The earliest you can start claiming Social Security checks is at age 62, which is likely to be bad news for early retirement enthusiasts because what happens when you retire at, say, 50 or 55 and cannot claim Social Security benefits until you're 62?

Also, the earlier you start claiming benefits, the less money you'll get. The optimal age to start claiming benefits is between the ages of 67 and 70 because you get more perks and no penalties.

So, the picture should be getting more apparent now.

- You're not getting exactly what you contributed.
- You cannot even claim benefits until you're really old.

And this will probably break your heart, but The Social Security Administration reports that retirement beneficiaries receive around 40% of their pre-retirement income on average.

So, you can expect to receive 40% of your current monthly earnings when you retire. This means that if you're struggling, barely getting by with what you currently earn, you might have a hard time when you retire except if you put a solid and effective retirement plan in place.

This is why, no matter what you do, you must never spend your career thinking your Social Security account will leave you in good shape for retirement. It's a trap many people have fallen into in the past, and you don't want to make this mistake too.

Caught Between a Rock and a Very Hard Place

Imagine being in your 70s and being worried sick all the time that you can't eat as well as you want – let alone pay your bills – because you did not have a retirement plan when you were younger and able to work.

Imagine being in your sunset years, completely ineligible for meaningful employment, not having enough money saved up to, say, start a business. Picture yourself watching the light and water bills get stacked up on your kitchen counter, fearful that your amenities will be cut off any time because you don't have the funds to take care of them.

And what's more – growing old is expensive – a lot more costly than being young. Ask anyone blessed enough to grow old, and they will affirm this. Your body isn't what it used to be; it doesn't heal up as fast as it used to, and you'll need to see a doctor most times to patch your health up where before you could pop a tablet or two and ride out your illness.

So, you'll need to be able to afford loftier medical bills as you're likely to be seeing doctors with more frequency than you are now. This is just one way in which growing old is expensive.

Think about all this – you'll not only have the same set of bills to take care of (water, electricity, etc.); you will also have more of those to foot, and all this without being able to earn a regular salary.

And let's not forget inflation, emergencies or unexpected life events, and economic fluctuations. When you retire, your paycheck will be cut in half (if you're relying solely on Social Security), but your expenses might even double.

Furthermore, if your income exceeds $34,000, you must pay taxes on 85% of your Social Security benefits. This income also includes taxable investment income.

It's daunting to head into your retirement years with little or nothing saved up. It's unfortunate, but most folks do not live too long after they retire because the worry wears them down. Life becomes too hard and unenjoyable, and they slowly give up on it. You do not want this to be your fate.

Retirement planning is a serious business and not something to put on the back burner. This is the other half of your life we're talking about. It's essential to remember that as you're working right now, you're not just working for now; you're also working for your future self.

Whatever income you're receiving right now is not only to cater to your current self, it's also supposed to cater to your future self, who will probably be too tired to work as hard or earn as much as you are currently.

Hence, developing a conservative financial plan that provides a reasonable lifestyle in your retirement, mainly your late retirement, shouldn't be considered an option but a basic necessity of life. No matter how old you are, it's never too early or too late to start planning for retirement. Regardless of how much of a mess you think your finances are right now, you can start planning for retirement.

This guide will teach you how to put your financial life in order. You will discover how to build a solid, fail-proof retirement plan that has worked for many others before you so that you will never have to spend a sleepless night fussing over how you'll eat, pay your bills, go on holiday, etc., as a senior.

It will help you avoid the mistakes that so many others before you have made so that your retirement years end up becoming the best years of your life.

Let's get started!

Chapter 1: How To Get Ready for a Retirement Plan

This chapter will help you understand your current and future needs during retirement to know how much you ultimately need. It will also aid you in determining the perfect time frame for you to start planning for retirement (the right time to start planning for retirement is right now, by the way, and this chapter will help you see why). This guide will also highlight crucial short, medium, and long-term goals, how they relate to retirement, and how to set them.

Aside from understanding the importance of a retirement plan, you will also discover the fundamental elements of getting your retirement plan set up and running.

With this said, it is important that we appropriately define a retirement plan first and cover its core aspects and elements so that we have a well-set-out, robust base to build the rest of this guide's content. So, without further ado, let's start from the top.

Understanding What a Retirement Plan Is

Retirement planning is simply putting effective systems and strategies to help you make the most of your retired life. By "systems and strategies," we mean money/cash-flow systems and policies. These will ensure you have enough money to live off of once you're retired and cannot bring home the bread as you used to when you were gainfully employed.

Let's break this down a little more:

You've spent your career working hard to create a comfortable life for yourself and your family. However, with retirement, you will no longer be able to take home a salary. Nevertheless, best believe that your bills will stay the same. You may be able to cut costs here and there and readjust your lifestyle, so it's less intensive as far as costs go, but there's only so much you can do about the usual bills.

You'll want to eat out every once in a while, go on holiday sometime, throw a party with your retired friends and reminisce, and so on. Basically, you'll want to keep living and not be forced to retract into a defensive, finance-deficiency-fueled shell. This is why a retirement plan is vital – it will allow you to keep living and not be a 75-year-old prisoner that cannot enjoy life because there's no money.

Retirement planning envisions all the costs and expenses as you get older, including the staple ones, like being able to keep your lights on and the faucets flowing, and prepares you for them.

Julia Kagan defines it as *"What one does to be prepared for life after paid work ends."*

However, retirement planning goes beyond just the financial aspect, albeit this is the most vital one. If your retirement plan is only focused on the income and expenditure aspects of your future life, you'll still have a good time with no financial worry; but what you have here is far too one-dimensional to be a real retirement plan. It is more of a pension plan than a retirement plan.

A pension plan only takes into consideration your financial future, i.e., your income vis-à-vis your expenditure. In contrast, a retirement plan is an all-encompassing plan that tries to anticipate all the changes that might occur in all aspects of your life so that you can be adequately prepared for them.

This includes changes to your health needs (we highlighted this in our introduction), lifestyle, living situation, relationships, the economy, and so on. As you grow older, your living dynamics will also change, and your retirement plan will be set up to accommodate these as well.

A retirement plan also considers your changing goals as you grow older – what it will take for you to live a happy and fulfilled life in retirement.

As such, a retirement plan is not just about money. It is mostly about money, make no mistake. Still, it is about more than that: your well-being, your happiness, your changing goals, your adjusted way of living, etc. It's about living comfortably – boldly, too – when you're retired. Your golden years should be years of comfort and enjoyment.

If you do decide to pick up an extra job to supplement your income after you retire, that should be something you do completely out of pleasure and because you feel you have more than enough energy and vigor to work. It should never be because you're tired of waiting for your kids to send you extra money since your pension can barely pay the bills.

When you retire, you deserve – yes, *deserve* – to be as relaxed, comfortable, and as happy as you can be. And a retirement plan is how you get there.

Let's move on to the following fundamental element of retirement planning that you need to understand – the stages of retirement planning.

But first...

Why do So Many Folks Not Plan for Retirement?

Why is it so hard to convince young people to set up a retirement plan? Here's what several ordinary, working-class Americans have to say on this one:

Dave Norris:

"I had my first legitimate job in a tire garage. It was a nasty, steamy job. We all congregated in the changing room at the conclusion of the workday to scour off as much grime and soot off of our bodies as we could. I had just turned nineteen. I gleefully yelled, "One year down," as I cleaned up on the evening of my one-year anniversary. "Only 45 more to go!"

"The elderly individuals cast me a dejected glance as they stated, "It seems like a great many years today, but it will be over before you realize it."

"Now, 45 years have passed since then. The veterans were correct. Although it feels like yesterday, you can never persuade a youngster that time can pass so quickly."

Chip Stites, Retired CFP:

"Why is it so challenging to communicate with someone who acts as though they're immortal and believes they are the center of the universe? (This will likely persist until the late thirties, even the early forties or longer). Or even that the turtle triumphs over the rabbit in the race? (The Tortoise and the Hare, an Aesop's Fable.)

"Because of their youth! People don't start to develop a perspective on life until their late 30s, 40s, or perhaps 50s."

A wonderful quote from Cicero that applies to this situation is, "Great things are not accomplished by muscle, speed, and skill, but by contemplation, the strength of character, and capacity for astute discernment; in these virtues, old age is generally not only not poorer, but it is even wealthier." Cicero – (106 – 43 BC)

"Another well-known example is the twenty-year-old who made investments of X dollars each month for ten years before stopping. And the friend who sees the account statement at the end of ten years exclaims, "Wow, I would like to start that!"

"Will the guy or girl starting a new account at thirty ever catch up to the person who started ten years ago and stopped at 30 if they earn and deposit the same amount?

"No!

However, young adults don't give a damn about this, do they? Youth is mostly wasted on the young, as the adage goes."

Terry Weaver has quite a unique perspective on this:

"Actually, I have a completely different perspective on this issue.

"I've discovered via my voluntary work that the typical American cannot perform two-digit math. It's similar to asking, "How many more pennies do I need if I have 50 and want 57? No, really. More than half of Americans are unable to answer the question correctly.

"So, I've arrived at the conclusion that Americans generally, not just 20-somethings, are incapable of understanding how to save and invest for retirement because they lack MATH skills. It is evident that our federal politicians are illiterate in math; otherwise, they wouldn't make the choices they are.

"Our nation faces a serious threat to its ability to preserve its position as a superpower if we can't repair our educational system."

The Stages of Retirement Planning

One of the essential facts to remember about retirement planning is that there are different planning stages with different strategies suitable for each step. We'll discuss these strategies in detail later, but this will give you a general idea.

First, we have the **young adulthood stage**, which is pretty much for people who have just started their careers or are within the first decade of their careers. These people will typically fall between the ages of 21 and 35.

Young adults may not have much money available for investing. Still, they have time to wait for investments to mature, a crucial and priceless component of retirement savings due to the compounding principle (more about this later).

The more time you have until retirement, the more interest you will be able to earn, thanks to the wonders of compounding. Even if you can only save and invest $50 a month towards your retirement, it will increase in value three times faster than starting at age 45.

There is no way to make up for lost time, even if you were to invest more money in the future. It's true that you can save up larger sums of money in the future, but you'll never be able to make up for all the lost time and potential income you would have earned if you started out earlier.

The second stage is the **early middle-life stage**, including people between the ages of 36 and 50.

Early mid-lifers tend to have more financial burdens compared to young adults. Financial obligations such as mortgages, student loans, insurance premiums, and credit card debt frequently appear in early middle age.

Nonetheless, saving and investing for retirement must continue at this age. In fact, this is the most crucial time to take retirement planning more seriously. These are some of the best years for aggressive saving because of the increased income and the time you still have to invest and earn interest.

Then, there's the third stage which we'll call the **late mid-life stage**, and covers people between 50 and 65. It's never too late for retirement planning, and even though it may seem like time is running out for these groups of people, there are some benefits of starting retirement planning at this age.

People in this category typically have more wages, usually because they occupy more senior positions at work or because some debts might have been paid off, like student loans, mortgages, etc., leaving them with more disposable income to save and invest toward retirement. However, late mid-lifers are limited in their investment choices because there's much less room for risk-taking, so they ideally have to go for more conservative and safer investment options.

So, you see, there are benefits no matter when you decide to start planning for retirement. Whether you're starting at 21 or 50, it's okay. The most important thing is that you start and have a solid retirement plan by the time you are ready to retire.

Next up, we look at the third fundamental element of retirement planning that you need to be in the know about – the most important aspects/elements of retirement planning.

Vital Aspects of Retirement Planning

As mentioned earlier, retirement planning doesn't just cover the income and expenditure part of your retirement. There are a lot of aspects that it helps you to plan for, such as:

1. Health Planning

Many people don't know this, but retirement planning also includes planning for health management. You're going to get older, and your health needs will change as you age, and health insurance may not be sufficient to cover those needs.

So, effective retirement planning involves taking into account your current lifestyle and trying to forecast what your health needs might be as you grow older. For example, if you're a heavy smoker, your retirement plan can include putting money aside to manage any common illnesses that heavy smokers might face in old age.

2. Homes

The single biggest asset most people hold is their house. What role does that play in your retirement strategy?

Retirement planning experts no longer view a home as having the same value as they once did because of the housing market catastrophe. Due to the prevalence of home equity loans and lines of credit (HELOCs), many homeowners are retiring with mortgage debts.

Another consideration after retirement is whether to sell your house. If you still reside in the house where you raised several children, it may be larger than you require, and the costs associated with maintaining it may be high. An objective assessment of your house and what to do with it should be part of your retirement plan.

If you decide to keep your home, the maintenance costs would also have to be factored into your retirement plan.

3. Estate Planning

What would happen to your assets after you pass away? This will also be included in your retirement plan under the estate planning section. Estate planning also includes strategies to shield your assets from estate taxes as much as possible. We will look at this in more depth in the very next chapter.

4. Tax Savings

Taxes become a significant issue once you reach retirement age and receive payouts. Your retirement accounts are generally subject to ordinary income tax. This means that the tax rate on any withdrawals from your regular 401(k) or IRA may be as high as 37%.

Since a Roth IRA and a Roth 401(k) allow you to pay taxes now rather than later upon exit, they should be carefully considered.

Conversion to Roth can make sense if you think your income will increase later in life. You can get assistance from an accountant or financial planner to navigate such tax considerations. We'll touch on this in the next chapter as well.

5. Insurance Protection

Asset protection is a crucial part of retirement planning. Also, you will have to navigate the frequently complex Medicare system as you age, which comes with higher medical costs.

Many people believe that the coverage offered by regular Medicare is insufficient, so they seek Medicare Advantage or Medigap policies to complement it. In addition, life and long-term care insurance should be deliberated.

You may want to consider annuities, a kind of policy that insurance companies provide. A pension and an annuity are very similar. An insurance provider accepts a money deposit in exchange for a fixed monthly payment. When determining whether an annuity is an appropriate choice for you, there are many different alternatives and factors to take into account.

Next up, we'll look at the fourth and final retirement planning fundamental element which is the set of challenges associated with retirement planning.

Retirement Planning Challenges

Before you get into the practical aspects of retirement planning, it's essential to understand some typical challenges people often encounter. A person could spend most of their adult life saving and investing towards retirement and still come short due to some retirement planning challenges.

As you already know, there are no certainties in life, which also goes for retirement planning. Whenever we engage in planning activities, we do it with the hope that everything stays ceteris paribus.

But in real life, that hardly ever happens. More often than not, something usually happens that will require us to adjust or make new plans. And that's the approach you should take toward retirement planning. Make brilliant plans, but ensure that your plan is flexible enough to accommodate future uncertainties.

Some common challenges that people often face in retirement include:

1. Family Emergencies

Sometimes, there might be incidents in the family that might require you to completely change the lifestyle that you planned to live in retirement.

For example, I once had clients, an elderly couple in their 80's, who unfortunately lost their daughter. So, they had to adopt her two kids.

That's two more mouths to feed that they didn't plan for before they retired. And because they couldn't raise the kids by themselves due to age-related difficulties, they had to hire help. They also had to make provisions for all future expenses relating to the kids, including their college funds.

No one hopes or prays for such disasters to happen. We all hope for the best, and it's always good to be positive. However, we must never be so naive that we fail to plan for the negatives.

2. Adult Children Challenges

Most parents can't bear to see their kids in trouble or needing help. If your kids encounter any future challenges, you're likely to be their first port of call when seeking help. If you have kids, making provisions for situations like this in your retirement plan is always a good idea.

3. Identity Theft

This is not something many people give much thought to, but we are in the digital age, and now, more than ever, your financial assets are vulnerable.

As you grow older, you might need more help from other people to help you make sense of digital technologies and innovations. One tiny error in judgment and your information could land in the wrong hands, and all your retirement savings stolen by internet scammers prowling the internet, looking for vulnerable people to steal from.

Again, you need to keep this in mind and plan for it. How do you guard against losing your investments and retirement savings to identity theft? If it ever happens, how do you insure your assets and protect yourself from the effects of such occurrences? Ponder on this.

4. Economic Uncertainties

Things like government policies, taxes, and inflation can put a dent in your retirement plan.

Let's take inflation, for instance. Since many retirees may be living on fixed incomes that cannot keep up with rising expenditures, higher inflation presents particular challenges for them. In addition, there is already above-average price inflation for many items and services that retirees consume the most.

Costs associated with health care, for instance, could be extremely high. According to HealthView Services, a 65-year-old couple in good health who retired in 2019 with Medicare Parts B and D and additional insurance coverage may anticipate paying $387,644 for healthcare expenses throughout their lives.

When making your plan, it's crucial to make provisions for potential economic or policy changes that can affect your retirement savings and investments.

5. Natural Disasters

We've seen things like this happen before, where retirees lose their homes to tsunamis, fire disasters, or storms.

And while most of them have insurance coverage for such disasters, the immediate inconveniences, such as finding a temporary place to stay, can still put a dent in your retirement funds if you don't make provisions for it.

6. Black Swan Events

There is always a chance of market fluctuations and "Black Swan" incidents, which can significantly affect financial markets when they happen. 9/11, the real estate bubble that caused the Financial Crisis, and the coronavirus epidemic are the best examples of black swan occurrences. In a nutshell, black swan events are those that defy prediction.

The impact of these events is more pronounced than ever before because nowadays, trading (stock, forex, cryptocurrency) is carried out online and at neck-breaking speeds amongst many participants worldwide, and online trading continues even after markets close.

The rise of social media has also sped up the process of decision-making. All of these have made financial markets more volatile than in the past.

7. Technological Advancements and Trends

The world keeps evolving and changing, and it doesn't look like it will slow down anytime soon. Look at trends in the real estate industry, for example. There's a growing trend of people living off-grid, buying tiny homes, and generally choosing to live in minimalist homes.

There are even innovations by companies like Boxbl that make portable, pre-fabricated homes. Now, assuming that these become the norm in the future and traditional homes lose their value, your home's value could also take a hit.

This is why retirement planning should be an ongoing exercise. You have to keep studying your environment and looking out for trends to keep adjusting your plans to fit into the trends.

8. Years Money Must Last

No one really knows how long they'll live; all we can do is forecast. A male, today in his mid-50s, has around a one-in-three chance of living to be 90, while a woman of the same age has about a 50% chance, according to the Society of Actuaries.

This implies that you may very easily spend the same number of years in retirement as you did in your working years. So you will need to get enough money to cover daily needs for perhaps 30 years or longer, which is challenging when you have few guaranteed income options.

What if you end up living longer than most people do?

What if you live well into your late 90s and in your retirement plan, you only made plans for up to the 80s?

Where's the money to sustain you going to come from?

Keep in mind that this stage of life is probably the most expensive because of personal care and medical costs.

9. Medical Costs

Speaking of medical costs, sometimes it's hard to put a number on them because you can't be 100 percent certain of the kind of healthcare needs you may have in retirement.

Up to this point, this book has indirectly addressed the most critical aspect of retirement: you need to start working on your retirement plan ASAP, like *now*.

The longer you can save up and set up systems and strategies to comprehensively set your life up and accord you comfort, freedom, boldness, and spontaneity, the more prepared you will be for retirement.

The more time you have to prepare, the better equipped you will be when the time comes. You'll have more time, energy, less pressure and ultimately more money to work with if you start now, as opposed to waiting even a year. The chapter on compound interest will really highlight these points. It will cover finances primarily, but you're smart enough to extrapolate these points to time, energy, vigor, extra planning, etc.

Now, with the fundamentals covered and the most important questions answered, let's dig in and learn how to prepare for a retirement plan.

Preparing Comprehensively for Your Retirement Plan

For many people, a fulfilling and enjoyable retirement entails different things. It can entail switching from a long and successful career to a fulfilling part-time job for you.

Or maybe you see yourself devoting more time to being with your loved ones, starting a small garden, or playing golf regularly. After you've decided what aspects of retirement would give you the most peace of mind, it's critical to understand how you will financially get there. We'll walk you through some quick (and enjoyable) steps to get you going.

Let's get started:

Step 1: Define Your Retirement

You most likely have a general concept of how you want to spend your retirement. Here's where you should list your goals, starting with the most crucial ones. Don't concentrate on the budget at this time.

Be as descriptive as possible while concentrating on ideas. For instance, list "excursions to the lakeside" or "guided tours of distant nations" in place of "travel." Replace "remain connected in the community" with "volunteer with my kids two days a week" when making a list of goals.

Try to keep this list to only your top 5 objectives. Keep a scrapbook or begin a journal in which you can describe your retirement goals.

Your retirement will become more solid and tangible the more specific you are. This will assist in keeping you concentrated on a manageable set of objectives, making each more feasible.

It's okay if your objectives are quite general or vague. You can just start by stating how you plan to spend your retirement and then flesh it out from there.

Be realistic: this list should exclude pointless expenditures. As you brainstorm, ensure all your financial necessities are addressed.

Step 2: Take Complete Stock of Your 'Assets'

You know how much money you make every month, what you've got in the bank, and what you have set aside for retirement. But what about the other non-traditional assets that might finance your retirement, though? Perhaps you restore automobiles or amass antiquities. You might be a skilled musician or have a book you're working on finishing.

Numerous interests and abilities, such as teaching piano, or trading antiques, might be leveraged into a viable source of income in your later years.

List every one of your interests and qualifications. List every one of your interests and unconventional "assets," regardless of how long or short your list is. Afterward, consider how you may turn those talents and interests into lucrative ventures.

Step 3: Evaluate Your Health — Now

You want to be as healthy as you can be to enjoy your retirement and your life, in general, to the fullest. And while very few of us look forward to visiting the doctor, a little preventive care can help.

Make an appointment for all your preventative care procedures, including a dental cleaning and yearly physicals. Work on a personalized plan to maintain or enhance your health and wellness together with your doctor at each visit.

Make a promise to eat well, exercise, and get adequate sleep. There is no need for healthy living to be complicated. Exercise can be enjoyable (anyone up for a walk on the beach?), and many healthy foods are tasty and filling.

Dedicate yourself to maintaining mental acuity through reading, puzzles, and brain games. Maintaining regular contact with your loved ones will keep you mentally and physically well and can help you fend off any retirement blues.

Step 4: Determine When to Collect Social Security

(Hint: Later Is Better!)

We've talked at length about Social Security and insisted on it not being your primary source of income when you retire. It is, at best, a crutch… but a critical one nonetheless, and one that could help prop you up.

The sum of your monthly payments will directly depend on when you decide to begin collecting Social Security. The advantage for both you and your family will increase the more time you wait to file for Social Security. We've already covered all this.

Think about this: a widow or widower whose spouse filed for Social Security at full retirement age or later is entitled to 100% of said benefits. Depending on when the spouse started claiming, a widower or widow whose spouse started receiving benefits early receives 71 percent to 99 percent.

You'll also be qualified for deferred retirement credits if you wait to file, which will enhance your benefits every year until you turn 70. Regardless of your situation—married, single, widowed, divorced— waiting to file usually pays off.

Step 5: Network Through Social-Media and Other Methods

Even after retirement, you still need to grow and manage your network. Actually, then more than ever, you will need to have a robust network of folks who will keep you rejuvenated in your retirement years.

Make the most of networking chances to show off your skills. Marketing yourself to others who could aid you in achieving your retirement goals (albeit not being cocky or arrogant while at it) is okay.

So, plan your retirement with a clear networking strategy in mind.

It can include organizing a morning meet-up group at a nearby coffee shop to brainstorm and discuss helpful ideas with other soon-to-be retirees or dedicating time each day "conversing" on Twitter or LinkedIn with individuals with similar interests and abilities, etc.

These activities will nurture meaningful connections, expanding your network and making your retirement years that much sweeter. Additionally, be ready to address questions (in your retirement plan) such as, "How could I put my skills and expertise to use, contribute part-time to, say, a charity institution or cause?" with concise, direct responses.

You are much likelier to create possibilities and opportunities for yourself if you're socially active both offline and online. So think about this one when preparing to put together a retirement plan.

Step 6: Figure Out How Frequently You Want (or need) to work

This is the classic cost-benefit equation: The goal of this guide is to ensure you are financially set for life by the time you retire (along with having other structures set up).

However, some of us are only now getting wise to have a retirement plan in our 50s, which does not leave enough time to save up to the point where absolute financial independence is achieved by the time the retirement years roll up.

If the above describes you, you will have to either stretch limited money and give up some retirement dreams or stay in the workforce (in some capacity) to help pay for those dreams.

As you write down your retirement goals, consider how much work may be necessary for your retirement years (hopefully, if it comes to it, you will only need to clock in part-time and in something that you love to do anyway.)

"Work" will signify different things to different people during retirement. In the previous step, you were encouraged to look at your interests. But you should consider your lifestyle and preferences, too.

Regardless, to make sure you effectively achieve your goals, you'll have to settle on how much time you want (or need) to spend working. It would be dangerous to wait until after retirement to make the choice. Fill out the details — including the hours to work per week. The earlier you get comfortable with this decision, the more secure you will be in your retirement planning.

Step 7: Create a Retirement Budget

Your budget should include:

- How much cash is being generated
- How much it will cost to achieve the objectives you chose in step 1
- The amount of debt you have

Start by keeping a record of your earnings and expenditure for a few months. Estimate the amount of money you'll require after retiring to support the lifestyle you've settled on.

You'll additionally need to examine your investments' financial situation. Invest in things you understand, spread your money among several different types of investments, and use low-fee options where possible.

If you have debt, make sure your budget includes regular payments to reduce it. Start implementing your budget after you have one that you are confident you can follow.

Step 8: Look for New Ways to Lower Expenses (Begin Saving More)

The time is now to explore new ways to minimize your spending, but that does not mean that all your additional money needs to be put into savings – what we're calling for here is balance.

Increasing your savings today by finding new ways to slash your expenses will improve your financial "readiness" by the time you retire. Make a list of your expenses first, and then explore ways to reduce them.

Perhaps you don't need three evenings of eating out per week or 100 cable TV channels when you only watch 6 of them. You can bring your retirement objectives and goals closer by reducing your monthly movie nights even by one.

Perhaps, you're good with plants and can save money by producing your veggies, which you can then put aside for retirement. Don't disregard your debt to increase your savings.

Reducing your debt today will make retirement less stressful. Paying off your smaller obligations first, no matter their interest rate is a common debt-reduction method that has worked for many people.

This particular method provides you with a feeling of fulfillment, as you will have managed to wipe off total debts and turn your focus on others. It affords you the confidence to take on the more prominent bills since you know you've got the resolve to pay them off.

Step 9: Prepare for the Unexpected

Very few folks anticipate the worst when they approach and enter retirement. But occasionally (actually, a lot more often than just "occasionally," if we're being honest), it does.

You won't be caught off guard if you start your preparations immediately. It will be easier for you to ride out any storm in your retirement years if you take the time to plan how you would handle everything from simple problems, like a leaky roof, to catastrophic ones, like a terminal disease.

Discuss potential issues with your family members, loved ones, or friends to get their perspective on them: how much should significant repairs cost? If someone in your family were unwell, what should be done, and how much care and attention would you like to see administered?

Step 10: Stick to Your Plan (This Book Will Help with That)

Sticking to your plan may be difficult, but it will be unquestionably rewarding. The most iron-clad approach to seeing the fruits of a plan/strategy is to stick to it right to the end.

Being creatures of habit, humans frequently go back into old routines after attempting a new line of action. This book will provide you with sufficient aid in averting that.

Next up, we look comprehensively at how much you need to retire.

Chapter 2: How Much do You Need to Retire?

The process of planning for retirement involves several steps and changes over time. You must create a financial safety net that will cover absolutely everything if you want to retire in comfort and security and also have plenty of fun while at it.

The latter one – the fun aspect – is a major reason you should focus on the critical stuff when making travel arrangements.

Mulling over your retirement objectives and just how long you've got to achieve them is the first step in retirement planning. Then it would be best if you considered several retirement account types that can aid you in raising the funds necessary to finance your future. You must invest the money you save for it to grow.

The final aspect of preparing is taxes: If you've accumulated tax benefits for the funds you've put into your retirement savings over the years, you'll face a substantial tax charge when you begin taking those funds out.

So, as you're saving for your future, there are strategies you can implement to reduce the retirement tax hit—and ways to carry on the process once the day comes when you finally stop working.

All of these topics will be covered in this guide. But this chapter will primarily focus on how much you need to save for retirement.

How Much Do You Need to Save for Retirement?

We all want to clearly understand how much money we should put aside before we begin calculating the figures for our retirement goals. Obviously, this will rely on various contextual variables, including annual salary and the age at which we intend to retire.

Although there isn't a set amount to save, most retirement experts suggest benchmarks like accumulating around $1 million or twelve years of your annual pre-retirement salary. Others advise following the 4% rule, which states that pensioners should not spend upwards of 4 percent of their retirement assets each year to guarantee a good retirement.

According to Ben Storey, director of Retirement Research & Insights at Bank of America, due to the numerous variables, even retirement experts can't really settle on a unanimous total cash figure. "Whatever each individual requires will vary greatly depending on a variety of things."

These variables include:

- Your present age
- The age at which you intend to retire, or may be required to retire, due to deteriorating health, losing a job, or other uncontrollable circumstances
- Your expected life expectancy based on your family history
- The amount you intend to spend after you retire
- Your projected sources of income in retirement

You might be shocked by how much money even modest accounts could possibly generate throughout retirement. The following instances show the amount that a 65-year-old could prudently withdraw during their first retirement year:

Savings value at age 65		Annual income from savings*
$300,000	⇨	$12,060/year

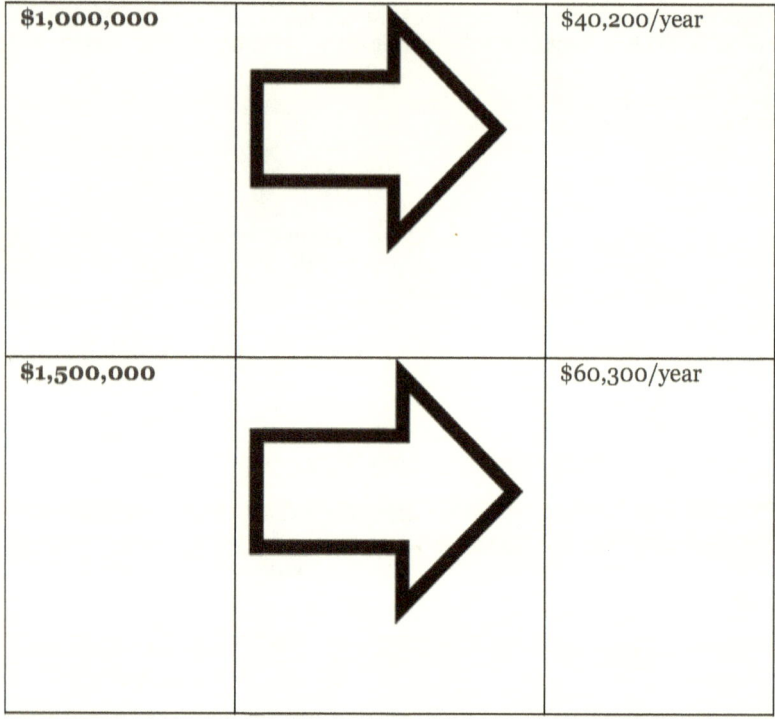

How much you save and invest, as well as how you use your nest egg when you retire, will determine how substantial your nest egg must be, and how long it might remain.

Here are a few things to think about when you choose what your personal savings target should be.

Factors to Consider

Evaluate some of the elements that will impact your retirement objectives when you start to think about retiring. What, for instance, are your family plans? Having a family is a major life ambition for many individuals, but raising children can severely diminish your savings. The kind of family that you want to have will therefore affect how you plan for retirement.

Likewise, it is important to consider your retirement plans, including any improvements or modifications you may need to make to your living space/house.

Traveling a lot is likely to deplete your savings and investments a lot faster as compared to staying put at home, despite the fact that it could be an exhilarating journey. On the other hand, relocating to a nation with a very low living cost can enable you to stretch your savings while still enjoying a high level of living.

The various kinds of tax-advantaged retirement funds should also be taken into account. The majority of Americans are eligible for social welfare, but these payments are rarely sufficient to cover the entirety their retirement needs.

While retirement funds were previously the standard for skilled workers, self-funded programs like 401(k), or IRA vehicles have essentially taken their place. Your retirement approach will be dependent on the kinds of tax-advantaged accounts you have access to because these come with a maximum contribution cap.

Following your consideration of these considerations, take the following actions to prepare your retirement:

1. **Understand Your Time Horizon**

The foundation for a successful retirement strategy will be hinged on your present age and anticipated retirement age. The greater the degree of risk that your portfolio is able to handle, the more time you have till retirement.

The bulk of your holdings can be in riskier, speculative investments, such as equities, if you are young and have more than 30 years till retirement. Despite equities having some level of volatility, over a long time, equities have outperformed many other financial investments – this includes bonds. What you have to note here is that the period is a long time (at least ten years).

As a rule, though; you should make sure your returns are higher than the inflation rate, as this will help you retain your purchasing power. "Inflation is just like the acorn. A towering oak tree can grow from a very small seed," says Chris Hammond, a financial counselor from Savannah, Tennessee, and the creator of RetirementPlanningMadeEasy.com.

"We have all heard about compounding interest on our money (this is covered in a chapter of its own in this guide), and want it to work for us," says Hammond. "Well, seeing as how inflation devalues your money, it is like 'compound anti-growth. Over the course of 24 years, a relatively little rate of inflation of 3% will reduce the value of your investment by 50%.

Despite the fact that it does not seem like much every year, over time it has a significant impact."

In general, your portfolio ought to be more concentrated on capital and income preservation as you get older. This entails placing a larger portion of your portfolio in safer investments, including bonds, which won't offer you the kind of yields you'll get from stocks, but are less volatile and give you income which you can dip into, to support yourself.

Additionally, you won't be as concerned about inflation. A 64-year-old who intends to retire the following year doesn't really worry as much about an increase in living expenses as a substantially younger person who has just started their career.

Your retirement strategy should be divided up into various parts. Assume a parent plans to retire in 2 years, send their child to college when they turn 18 and relocate to Florida. The investing strategy should therefore be divided into 3 time periods, from the standpoint of developing a retirement plan: the 2 years leading up to retirement (contributions are made to the retirement plan), saving for, and paying for college, and residing in Florida (steady cash withdrawals to foot living expenses).

To choose the best allocation method, a multi-stage retirement plan should take into account different time horizons and the subsequent liquidity necessities. More so, when your time horizon shifts over time, you ought to be rebalancing your portfolio.

2. Determine Retirement Spending Needs

You can determine the necessary amount of a retirement portfolio by having reasonable expectations about your post-retirement spending patterns. The majority of respondents think their annual budget will only be between 70% and 80% of what it was before retirement.

Such an assumption is generally shown to be unfounded, particularly if the mortgage is still owed or if unanticipated medical costs arise. It is not uncommon for retirees to spend up to five years' worth of savings in the early days of retirement by simply going on bucket list vacations and purchasing items they have wished to buy for a long time.

"I believe the ratio ought to be nearer to 100% for retired folks to have sufficient resources for retirement," says David G. Niggel, CEO of Key Wealth Partners LLC in Lititz, Pennsylvania.

Each year, living costs rise, particularly healthcare costs. Adults who are retired will have to save and invest more because they will need higher income, for a longer duration of time.

Retired individuals have much more time for travel, sightseeing, shopping, and other pricey hobbies because they are, by definition, not working 8 plus hours each day. Setting precise retirement spending targets aids in your planning process, since higher spending in the future necessitates greater savings now.

"Your rate of withdrawal is one factor—if not the biggest one—in the lifetime of your retirement assets. The amount of money you withdraw annually and how you finance your account will depend on how well you predict your retirement expenses."

According to Kevin Michels, CFP, EA, money manager and director of Medicus Wealth Planning in Draper, Utah, "if you understate your spending, you easily outlive your portfolio. Conversely if you overstate your expenses, you run the danger of not enjoying the kind of lifestyle you desire to have in retirement."

When making retirement plans, it's important to take your longevity into account to avoid outliving your savings. The average human life expectancy is rising.

Additionally, if you plan to buy a home or pay for your kid's education after retirement, you may need more revenue than you think. The total retirement plan must take these expenses into account. To ensure you are on pace as far as your savings go; keep in mind to revise your retirement plan at least once a year.

Here are the current financial habits of older Americans:

	Ages 50-64	Ages 65-74	Ages 75 and older
Housing	45.9%	44.9%	45.6%
Food	11.0%	11.2%	11.2%
Health	7.8%	9.6%	10.6%
Clothing	2.9%	2.9%	2.7%
Transportation	13.9%	12.0%	9.7%
Entertainment	10.2%	10.5%	8.3%
Other	4.7%	5.4%	6.3%

Remember that there might be savings elsewhere even though some expenses, like health care, may rise in retirement. "Researchers have discovered that after retirement, individuals devote more time meticulously planning their shopping trips and cooking at home, for instance. Their living costs decrease for products like these," says Storey.

3. Keep in mind all of the income sources that can help cover your expenses

Remember that the cash amount you choose to save and invest by yourself is simply one part of your future income in retirement as you think about how much cash you may actually need then.

Social Security will be the primary source of retirement income for many Americans. Social Security is unlikely to disappear in the future, even if benefit amounts are decreased.

Also, keep in mind that you may have access to additional streams of income, in the future, such as the funds in your personal and workplace retirement funds, annuities, pensions, revenues from the sale of your business or home, rental income, and inheritances.

Working in retirement: expectations vs. reality

Be reasonable with your expectations if you intend to work when retired so you are perhaps able to save less money today and live a little. Employee Benefit Research Institute's (EBRI) annual Retirement Confidence Survey has repeatedly shown that American workers are much more likely to envision working in retirement than actually doing so.

According to the most recent EBRI research, 72% of workers intended to continue working after retirement, compared to only 30% of retired folks who currently claim to be employed for pay.

Knowing your income and costs after retirement might help determine how much money you would need to take out of your savings and investments each year. However, when your financial target is decades away, it can be challenging to translate that objective into a reasonable figure to invest in now.

Consider incorporating the savings multiples below as a guideline for replacing your income in retirement. This is based on findings from Bank of America's Financial Wellness Tracker, a trademarked evaluation that determines a financial wellness score centered on where an employee is at today:

For instance, Jane, 35, who makes $70,000 a year, may simply multiply her present salary by 1.4 to compare it to her savings to evaluate how well she is saving compared to other people in her age group. Therefore, she would need to save $98,000 ($70,000* 1.4) so far to stay up with the "top" investors and savers in her equivalent wage group.

The difference that 1% can make

A small change in savings can give you substantially more after 30 years.

Any money you set aside today for long-term investments and savings could have a significant impact later on. "Even a 1% boost might mean a lot over time if you need to save more," he advises.

4. Calculate the After-Tax Rate of Investment Returns

The after-tax real return rate must be computed to determine whether it is feasible for your portfolio to generate the income you need to retire once the predicted time horizons and expenditure requirements have been established.

Even for longer-term investing, a mandated return rate of more than 10% (before taxes) is typically unattainable. Because low-risk retirement portfolios mainly consist of low-yielding fixed-income investments, this return criterion decreases as you age.

Let's put this into actual figures:

You're dependent on an excessive 12.5% return if, for instance, you need $50,000 in income but have a retirement portfolio totaling $400,000, presuming there is no taxation and the maintenance of the portfolio balance.

Early retirement planning has several benefits; for instance, your portfolio can be expanded to ensure a reasonable rate of return. The predicted return with a $1 million gross retirement equity investment would be 5%, which is considerably fairer.

Investment returns may be taxed based on the kind of retirement account you have. As a result, the actual return rate should be determined after taxes. However, one of the most critical steps in retirement planning is figuring out your tax situation when you start withdrawing money.

5. Evaluate Investment Goals vs. Risk Tolerance

The most crucial phase in retirement planning, whether you or a qualified financial expert is tasked with making the investment selections, is a proper portfolio allocation which leads to a balance between concerns of risk aversion and return objectives.

How much risk are you prepared to accept in order to achieve, even fast-track, your goals?

Should money be saved in risk-free treasury bonds to cover necessary expenses?

Ensure that you're at ease with the risks that are being taken as far as growing your portfolio goes and are aware of what is essential and what is optional. Founder of 7Twelve Portfolio in Springville, Utah, Craig L. Israelsen, Ph.D., offers this advice:

"Don't be a 'micromanager' who reacts to daily market noise. When the varied mutual funds in the portfolio have a poor year, add extra money to them," says Israelsen.

"'Helicopter' investors are more likely to overmanage their portfolios. Don't give up on the mutual fund that you're upset with this year; it can turn out to be the greatest performer in the following year."

According to John R. Frye, who is a senior advisor at Carnegie Investment Counsel, "*Markets will undergo extended cycles of down and up and, if you're making investments you won't need to tap into for forty years; you can bear to see the portfolio value climb and drop with those inevitable cycles.*"

"Buy, not sell, when the market falls. Refuse to succumb to anxiety. You would want to buy clothes if they were 20% discount, right? Why not do the same if stocks went on sale for a 20% discount?"

6. Stay on Top of Estate Planning

Another crucial element in a well-rounded, comprehensive retirement plan is estate planning, and each component necessitates the expertise of various experts in that industry, such as accountants and lawyers.

A retirement plan and an estate plan require the consideration of life insurance. A sound estate plan and life insurance coverage guarantee that your assets are transferred according to your preferences and that your nearest and dearest won't face financial hardship after your passing. A well-thought-out plan also helps prevent a pricey and frequently drawn-out probate procedure.

Another essential step in the process of estate planning is tax preparation. The tax consequences of giving assets vs. leaving them through the estate administration must be evaluated if you want to leave money to charity, relatives, or friends.

A typical retirement plan investing strategy is predicated on generating returns that cover annual living expenditures adjusted for inflation while maintaining the portfolio's value. The portfolio can then be given to the decedent's beneficiaries. It would help if you spoke with a tax advisor to choose the best strategy for the specific person.

According to Mark T. Hebner, founder and CEO of Index Fund Advisors Inc. in Irvine, California, and author of Index Funds: The 12-Step Recovery Program for Active Investors, "estate planning will change during an investor's lifetime."

Powers of attorney, as well as wills, are things that should be done early on. Trust might play a significant role in your financial strategy once you start a family.

How you want your money distributed later in life will be crucial regarding expenses and taxes. Hebner continues, "Making preparations and managing this component of your overall economic strategy can be facilitated by partnering with a fee-only estate-planning attorney."

Key Takeaways

1. When preparing for retirement, it's essential to think through time horizons, budget approximations, necessary after-tax yields, tolerance for risk, and estate planning.

2. Take advantage of compounding by beginning your retirement planning as early as possible.

3. Investors who are younger and nearer to retirement ought to be more risk-averse in their investment decisions.

4. Retirement strategies vary over time, demanding periodic portfolio reassessments and apprises to estate plans.

5. Retirement preparation will consider your profession, the number of dependents, retirement age, and post-retirement objectives.

So, How Much Must you Save to be Comfortable in Retirement?

One general guideline is to keep aside 15 percent of your gross annual revenue each year. Savings would start in your 20s and continue throughout your working years in an ideal world.

The Bottom Line

Planning for retirement is becoming more and more of a personal responsibility. Few workers, particularly those in the private sector, can rely on an employer-provided, benefit-defined pension. When you move to defined contribution plans, like 401(k)s, you take over management of the investments from your employer.

Finding a balance between reasonable yield expectations and a desirable living level is among the most challenging components of developing a thorough retirement plan. The best course of action is to build an adaptable portfolio that can be routinely modified to reflect shifting market trends and retirement goals.

Next, we look at why having a retirement plan is very important.

Chapter 3: Why Is Having a Retirement Plan Important?

Not too long ago, a buddy of mine – let's call him Joe – inquired about the importance of retirement planning. Chances are high that you've asked yourself the same thing too.

Joe has a solid education and a rewarding career. He is busy, and just like you, he didn't feel he had enough hours in his day to take on one of his most significant decisions a retirement planning.

Furthermore, despite having access to 15 of the most outstanding retirement channels on the market, he was unsure where to begin or whether he should begin.

Initially, Joe was hesitant to take on retirement planning owing to limited time and a sense of being overburdened. But he quickly discovered that everyone, regardless of income or degree, has to prepare for their retirement for various reasons.

To begin with, retirement could last for much longer than you expect it to. For instance, a 65-year-old married woman in 2022 has a 50 percent probability of living to 90 years old, as per Money Guide!

You may live a lot longer than you originally thought and if you're ill-prepared, you'll outlast your retirement savings and have a very miserable time towards the end of your life. Below, is a life expectancy table to drive our point home:

Life Expectancy Table

Probability Chance you will live to age shown	Mark Lives to Age		Katherine Lives to Age	
	Non-Smoker	Smoker	Non-Smoker	Smoker
50%	88	81	90	83
40%	90	83	92	85
30%	92	85	94	87
20%	95	87	97	89
10%	98	90	100	92

The above table brings fantastic news if you've planned for retirement beforehand. However, if you did not/do not prioritize retirement preparation, the thought of living a longer life may be very unsettling, as you very well could be left with no money only a few years into retirement and have no means of making some.

The typical Social Security payment in 2022 is also around $1,500, which is not nearly enough to maintain many people's pre-retirement standards of living. Simply put, social security benefits do not really give you the money you need for a financially secure retirement.

We've already said much about social security and why it shouldn't be your primary means of income in retirement age. It is, at best, a crutch (albeit, an important one that you should leverage alongside your designated retirement savings and investments).

Medicare, the leading insurance program for retirees, does not cover the rising costs of healthcare for many older adults as well. A person who turns 65 this year faces a 70% probability of requiring long-term nursing services – since health gets increasingly fragile the older you get. And as women get closer to the end of their lives, they often require more than 3 years of supported care. Only 20% of people 65 years old today will not need long-term supported care.

Do you see what we are trying to get at here? A sound retirement plan is as crucial as ever, especially now that we are projected to live longer than at any other point in history.

You have a much higher likelihood of retiring in a comfortable position, optimizing your income sources so that you can lead the lifestyle you want—if you put together a proper retirement plan, preferably starting immediately.

Retirement Planning is VITAL

Here are the most compelling arguments on why retirement planning isn't just essential but vital:

1. You do not know that which you do not know

You undoubtedly have a wealth of knowledge in a variety of areas – at your age, this is pretty much a given. But there are dozens of variables that can affect your capacity to preserve financial stability regarding retirement planning.

This means that you lack the knowledge and experience required to recognize the crucial queries and solutions that can support a good retirement since you haven't retired before nor experienced what things are like on the other side of life.

Retirement planning may fill in the blanks and provide answers to essential questions and concerns such as:

- What crucial tax, financial, and investment facts should I consider when making plans?
- If I would like to save more, what retirement accounts must I take into account?
- Am I a spouse who qualifies for social security benefits?
- Should I consider converting to a Roth? (we'll cover the Roth IRA later)
- What matters should I take into account when the economy or market is struggling?
- I have a dormant 401(k): Should I roll over or stay put?
- What financial matters should I think about before the year is over?
- When should I begin receiving social security?
- Do I need life insurance today?
- What is the ideal combination of investments or mutual funds?
- Should I take a lump amount of my pension?
- How much revenue can my portfolio produce once I retire?
- Which retirement funds ought I use first when I retire?
- How do I lessen my portfolio's volatility?

2. Better health owing to lower stress levels

The most significant cause of stress is having money issues. We all know this, just as we all know money runs the world and makes most things, if not all things, possible.

Over 70% of adults, per the American Psychiatric Association, are constantly fretting and stressing about money, which can harm your physical and mental health.

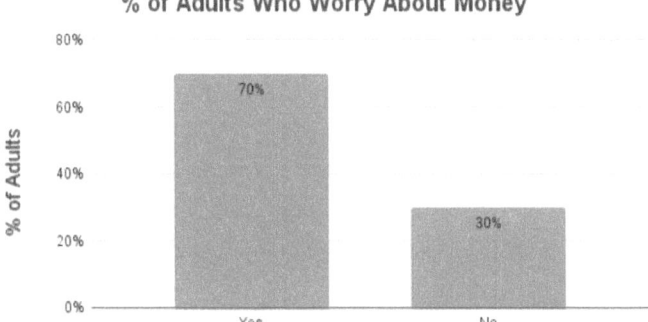

Do you worry about money?

Physical ailments, including diabetes, migraine headaches, heart disease, and poor sleep, are all associated with financial stress. Additionally, worrying about money can lead to anxiety and depression, robbing you of the serenity you need to enjoy the present. And remember, this serenity will be significant when you're older and retired, as your mental and physical health will be much more fragile then.

You can improve your overall financial well-being and, in turn, improve your physical and mental health by taking prudent financial actions today to start getting your retirement planning well on track.

3. The Average Life Expectancy Continues to Raise

We've already touched on this. Let's touch on it a little more, as there is more to it:

The fact that humans are now, on aggregate, living considerably longer than ever before is perhaps the foremost reason you ought to start saving for retirement.

Your retirement savings will need to be increased if you expect to live a longer life. Given that the median American lifespan is fast approaching 80 years old (which is amazing if you think about it), you will want a sizable sum of money stashed away to retire comfortably.

This is particularly true given that, even though the life expectancy on average is now close to 80, a considerable amount of us can expect to live even longer. If you are fortunate enough to fall into the above-average category, you will need to extend your retirement funds beyond what you (and most experts) had anticipated.

This calls for greater savings and longer-term planning. Your prospects of saving enough money for retirement to last you until the very end are better the sooner you start.

To put it simply, plan for a longer life expectancy rather than the usual one.

4. Relying on a Pension or Social Security Is Too Risky

We've also touched on this one, and we'll iron it out a little more here.

While Medicare's low-cost health insurance and Social Security's monthly benefits are available to you after you reach retirement age, it is highly unlikely that these benefits will be sufficient to provide you with the pleasant retirement you would like.

Your retirement savings will enhance your Social Security benefits and act as a backup plan in the event that Medicare and Social Security are ever cut.

Social Security and Medicare should not be your only sources of retirement income, and this is a point we have belabored up to this point. Pensions – which have also mostly become quite insipid with regard to providing financial propping up, owing to higher rates of inflation and other things – could not/will not be sufficient to support the kind of living to which you have been accustomed.

If you anticipate needing long-term care in the future, perhaps owing to a health condition, you should plan for it properly via a retirement plan. Your retirement assets could serve as a safety net to pay for nursing homes or other forms of care that Medicare might not (strike that; will not) cover entirely.

5. Send Less Money to Uncle Sam

Nobody enjoys having to pay more taxes than required. In fact, it is entirely unnecessary, not to mention completely useless, for apparent reasons. Also, this is money your kids and grandkids could use to have a happier life.

But unfortunately, if you aren't diligent, needless taxes can (and will) wipe out a significant portion of your retirement savings and investments. Aggressively minimizing those taxes (legally, of course) is a critical factor in retirement planning.

You must develop a tax plan for retirement, starting during your earning years, and educate yourself as much as you can on taxes and how to minimize them. Also, understand that once you're retired, your tax planning will be very different from when you were working. They are both similar, but you should approach them quite differently.

When you're working, you will likely have no authority or control over your income at your job, but your income is still very steady at the very least. As such, finding tax deductions and credits to lower your taxable income is crucial.

Contributing to your employer's 401(k) plan can cut your tax payments, saving you money if you are still growing your savings and investments.

Suppose you do not participate in an employer-sponsored retirement plan. In that case, you could be eligible to deduct your regular contributions to a Qualifying IRA up to the Annual Limit ($6,000 in 2022, or $7,000 if you are over 50).

TRADITIONAL IRA & ROTH IRA CONTRIBUTIONS	
Total Contribution Limit	$6,000
Catch Up (Age 50+)	$1,000

You should also consider using a Roth IRA, a Mega-Back Door Roth IRA, or a back-door Roth IRA to create a tax-free savings account.

Lower earners might even be eligible for the Saver's Credit, further lowering your tax obligation. You can qualify for a tax credit worth 10 percent to 50 percent of your retirement fund contributions based on your adjusted gross earnings and filing status.

You will also need to know how to lower your state income tax in whichever state you are in.

More control over your sources of income will increase your chances of lowering your taxes after retirement. From a tax planning perspective, you should have three categories or income sources in retirement:

- Tax-Deferred - Includes 401(k)s, social security, pension plans, and pre-tax IRAs.

- Tax-Free - Includes Health Savings Accounts (HSAs), Roth IRAs, and Municipal bonds.

- Tax-Managed - Includes standard brokerage accounts with such tax-efficient investments as index funds.

Concerning your retirement years, diversification of your sources of income in retirement could help you avoid paying tens, if not hundreds, of thousands of dollars in tax charges because it is impossible to foresee how taxes will change in the future.

Basically, try your best to have a very diversified portfolio and not have all your retirement investments and income tied to just a couple of vehicles. It then becomes effortless for Uncle Sam to swoop in and take out as much of your hard-earned money as possible.

As is very clear by now, tax reduction is a significant factor in retirement planning.

6. Big-picture Context Will You Make Superior Financial and Career Decisions

As you become older, life presents you with several significant questions. The solutions to these questions will rarely ever be straightforward. The truth is that the answers are frequently gray areas.

For instance:

- Should you continue with your current business or establish your own?

- Is it a good idea to take on a new college degree or job path in your latter years of employment?

- Should you fund or at least find another means to pay for your child's college?

- Can you be able to afford a beachfront vacation home?

These life choices shouldn't or cannot be undertaken in a vacuum because they have a significant financial impact. Knowing your retirement plan's status gives you the critical context needed to make essential decisions with assurance, especially when you can harness the power of compound interest (covered in a separate chapter of its own) to perform miracles for you.

7. Enjoy a Happier Marriage

To no one's surprise, financial problems are one of the main reasons for divorce. The incapacity to work toward a shared financial objective, excessive debt, and misaligned financial priorities are all factors that lead to marital conflict.

Retirement planning eliminates some significant sources of conflict in marriages when both partners share the same goals. When you remove money from the retirement equation, you can concentrate on making more enjoyable, less pressure-fueled choices and decisions, such as where you would like to retire.

Your marriage will benefit significantly from working with a financial expert who can offer unbiased, non-emotional advice.

8. Forced Early Retirement Will No Longer be a Scary Prospect

If it is in your plans to retire at 55, then that's terrific, and more power to you for wanting to retire early and live out your dreams; when it's not, however, it can be terrifying if you are forced to retire early.

Unfortunately, almost half of all retired folks in the current US population did not choose to retire. A smaller number of people had to step away from their paid jobs early to care for a parent or spouse who was ill or elderly, whereas the majority were let go at work or compelled by factors they couldn't ignore to quit their jobs.

If you have a retirement plan in place, you will be in a way better position if, for some reason, you have to leave your job before you'd planned.

Having money saved up for retirement affords you additional options, not to mention time, to revise your plans should you need to leave work earlier, even if your nest egg isn't fully built up as you would like it to be.

9. Retirement Is the Time to Check Off Your Bucket List, and You Need Financial Ability for This

You know that long list of places you've always wanted to go to and activities you've always wanted to try?

It's more than likely that you'll have obligations at home and work during your professional career and early years, making checking off your bucket list very challenging.

Often, some factors hold you back, whether related to your profession, raising a family, or other situations and events and circumstances in your life. But as long as you've made the proper plans with regard to retirement, you will no longer be held back and will be able to live out your dreams.

Retirement will be the ideal time to pursue those locations and experiences you have dreamed of for so long – it is only then that you can participate in activities you couldn't during your employment days.

One perk of retirement planning is that it enables you to live completely in the present once you are retired. You are no longer concerned with returning to your job or anything else related to it. You can use your time carefree.

Retirement is frequently the time to realize whatever life goals you may have had, but only if you meticulously planned during your working years. Otherwise, you could find yourself skimping on some experiences and omitting some things from your bucket list because your finances are not in good enough shape to support them.

You will have an easier time achieving these goals and reducing stress by having a sound financial retirement plan in place. Your finances will liberate you rather than constrain you if you have a healthy retirement fund.

10. Your Future May Have Considerably More & Greater Financial Obstacles Than Your Present or Past Have/Had

It's crucial to understand that you might face financial hitches in future, some of which may be even greater than anything you've had to contend with up to this point.

Most of us, and rightly so, have a positive view on our financial situation and believe that things will get better in the future, but this optimism is really not something you should count on.

Retirement planning is essential because there is no way to predict the future. When you have a sound retirement strategy in place, follow through to ensure you have rock-solid insurance.

And even if your retirement money will be available as a feasible safety net, if needed, you must work extra hard to fight the desire to use them if you get caught up in financial problems later, before you are retired.

You should save your retirement funds for when you actually retire because there are occasionally penalties for dipping into them, in addition to depleting them.

This shouldn't make you lose hope and optimism as far as retirement goes, but it should highlight how crucial having a proper retirement plan is. Your retirement plan will put you in the greatest position to deal with unforeseen speed bumps and financial difficulties that may lie ahead once you are retired.

11. You Will Never Have to Worry About Being a Burden to Your Kids

Do you know what the "sandwich generation" is? Have you heard of the term?

The sandwich generation describes those folks tasked with supporting their parents and their children at the same time.

About 44 percent of middle-aged individuals with kids at home have, at the least, one parent who may require care; 15 percent are full-fledged sandwich generation members who are saddled with supporting both parent(s) and their kids financially. This is a depressing situation, and you need to do everything you can to avoid making your child part of the sandwich gen.

Saving money for future medical and probable long-term care expenses is part of a complete retirement strategy, which you should be looking for. You won't need to ask your family to help out when you have a plan to take care of your expenses after you retire.

12. You Get to be a Super Cool Grandparent

A sound retirement plan will not only prevent you from burdening your children but also equips you with the means to be a wonderful grandparent.

Wouldn't it be lovely to welcome your entire family at your huge vacation house every year or take them on a fun annual vacation?

Even if your grandparenting objectives are perhaps a little more modest, having a sufficient income allows you to at least visit more frequently and be available for all of their significant occasions.

You can also use the money to pay for their university tuition or to get them some amazing birthday presents; perhaps even buy them their first car. Having a close connection with your grandkids will not (and should not) be hampered by money, especially when you've lived so long and worked so hard.

13. Continue your legacy of charitable giving

Most retirees tend to reduce their living costs in retirement but keep up their charitable giving routines.

If you've always given generously to charity while employed, it's likely imperative for you to keep doing so even when your working days are behind you.

Here are three ways in which retirement financial planning might maximize your charitable giving:

- It aids in generating the revenue required for lifelong philanthropic giving.
- It helps ensure that your legacy objectives are met through your estate plan.
- If properly laid out, it enables you to lessen your tax obligation.

A solid charity distribution strategy, outside the purview of this guide, can be a great tactic to help you maximize your philanthropic donations and keep helping people who need it.

Bonus: Set Up a Retirement Plan to Avoid Running Out of Money in Retirement

The idea of outlasting your resources is one of the most terrifying things you can imagine. If your portfolio is not maintained effectively, even one that appears suitable for your requirements and needs, it may not be sufficient, especially if market conditions and trends fluctuate.

Planning for retirement is crucial because it will prevent you from facing financial difficulties later in life. Your strategy will assist you in determining the return rate you require on your assets, the appropriate level of risk, and the maximum amount of income you can safely take out from your portfolio.

You'll have the appropriate amount saved up when your retirement comes up if you collaborate with a competent financial advisor that is specialized in retirement investment planning. Additionally, your assets will be handled in a fashion that guards against the unanticipated, so you are never caught short/off guard in an emergency.

This is the ultimate peace of mind.

Bottom Line

As you can clearly see, retirement planning is crucial for various reasons.

You need to be proactive if you want to reach your retirement goals. The earlier you begin retirement planning, the better your retirement will be in the long run.

There are dozens and dozens of ways that can help you maximize the next three decades, or more, of your life if you are close to retiring. This guide covers the most optimal of these.

Next up, we look at how to start saving for retirement.

Chapter 4: How to Start Saving for Retirement

The majority of Americans fall woefully short with regard to saving for retirement. As per the Federal Reserve, about two-thirds of non-retired individuals are apprehensive about their ability to reach their retirement savings objectives. Also, roughly a quarter of all adult Americans have nothing saved up for retirement whatsoever.

Do not let those figures depress you, however. If you are worried about retirement and the requisite savings you're trying to muster or haven't started setting aside money for retirement just yet, take a breather. Regardless of where you're at in life or how much money you are able to/need to invest, this guide will help you get on track.

And if you've already started saving for retirement, we'll teach you how to get the most out of your approach by utilizing various retirement accounts.

But before we look at the individual steps, here are some points we need to put across that supplement everything else covered in this chapter and help you be more prudent as you save up for retirement.

Vital Tips on Saving Up for Retirement

To start saving for retirement, consider the following essential tips:

1. **Focus on starting today**

Start saving right away if you can, especially if you are just starting to set money aside for retirement and garner compound interest—the capacity of your investments to produce earnings that are then reinvested to create their own earnings.

The sooner you can start, the better placed you will be, according to Greenberg.

Even a minimal investment at the beginning could have positive effects after decades of having compound interest fan its growth. A 25-year-old who starts saving at age 25 and puts away $75 per month will have more assets at age 65 than a 35-year-old who starts saving $100 a month, even though they are investing less each time.

Retirement Planning

A lesser investment over a more extended period will significantly impact your investment outcomes more than a greater investment over a shorter time frame.

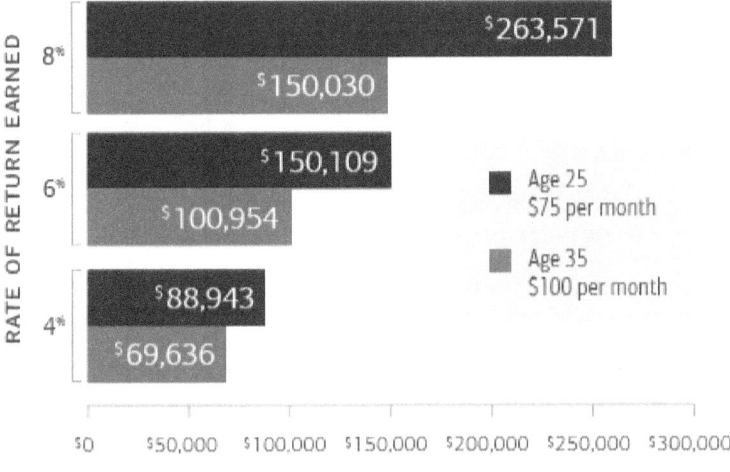

VALUE BY AGE 65

2. **Meet Your Employer's Match**

If your employer is up for matching your 401(k) plan contributions, you should make at least the minimum amount in contributions necessary to fully benefit from the match.

An employer might, for example, assure to match 50 percent of employee 401(k) contributions to, say, 5 percent of your salary. This means, if you make $50,000 each year and put $2,500 into your retirement account, your employer will contribute an additional $1,250. It's free money, in essence. Don't just let it stew on the table; match it, and the rewards down the line will be amazing.

3. **Open an IRA**

Think about opening an individual retirement account (IRA) to help you grow your nest egg. A standard IRA or a Roth IRA are your two alternatives. Depending on your earnings and whether you or your partner/spouse qualify for a company retirement plan, a traditional IRA might be the best option for you.

Tax deductions for commitments to a traditional IRA are possible, and any investment returns have the potential to grow utterly tax-deferred until withdrawals are made in retirement.

A Roth IRA can be a smart option if you fall under the phased-out, modified, adjusted gross income restrictions determined by your fed tax filing status. A Roth IRA is financed with after-tax payments. Consequently, the distributions and potential gains are tax-free once you reach the age of 59½, assuming that your account has been active for a minimum of 5 years.

4. Take advantage of catch-up contributions if you're age 50 or older

Seeing as yearly payments/contributions to IRAs and 401(k) plans are capped, it's crucial to start saving as early as possible. The positive news is that you become eligible for catch-up payments to IRAs and 401(k)s, beginning with the calendar year in which you turn 50.

As such, suppose you haven't been capable of saving up as much for retirement as you wanted over the years. In that case, catch-up contributions may help you make amends.

5. Rein in Your Spending

Check your spending plan and pare it down. You can save cash by bargaining for a lower vehicle insurance policy or carrying your lunch to work instead of purchasing it.

You can use Merrill's cash flow calculator to determine where your funds are going and where you can cut back so that you have more revenue to put away or invest.

When you are finally ready to retire, the amount you have can greatly depend on the amounts you direct to your retirement plan today. Assuming a $50,000 salary, even upping your retirement contribution rate from 4 percent to 6 percent over the course of 30 years will add well over $101,000 to your retirement nest egg.

With this covered; here are the seven most vital steps to develop your personal retirement investing strategy:

How to Start Saving for Retirement, Step by Step

Step 1: Set Your Retirement Savings Goal

Calculating the amount that you will need to set aside for a down payment on a house or a car is not difficult. On the other side, saving for retirement is a much greater, more difficult personal finance goal— it can (and very likely will) feel much more challenging to accomplish it perfectly.

There are numerous factors to take into account.

How much money will you require for travel?

Could you possibly incur high medical costs?

When will you completely stop working?

How long are you really going to live?

Most of us should start saving roughly 15% of our income starting at age 25 if we intend to retire by age 62, per the Center for Retirement Research at Boston College.

Starting later means you would need to save more, cut back on spending, or put in more hours. For instance, if someone started saving at age 35, they might theoretically fund a decent retirement by setting aside 24 percent of their earnings until they are 62 or 15 percent until they are 65.

Let's look at how to put a finger on your retirement needs:

a) Use the 25x Rule to Calculate Your Retirement Needs

The 25x rule can be used to set a more specific goal for yourself if you have a clearer understanding of your anticipated annual retirement spending. Calculate your anticipated yearly expenses for retirement, then multiply that sum by 25.

According to the 25x rule, you would need a sum total of $1.25 million in savings to comfortably retire if you anticipate $50,000 in yearly costs, for instance.

The 4 percent safe withdrawal rate serves as the foundation for this heuristic. Going by the 4 percent rule, you can safely remove 4 percent of your investment portfolio in the first year of retirement and then continue taking the same amount, with inflation adjustments each year, to avoid using up your assets too quickly.

b) Determine Your Monthly Savings Rate

Discover the amount you'll need to save annually to attain your overall retirement savings target using a retirement savings calculator. And while historically, rates of return in the market have been higher, estimate them at a prudent 6% annually, just to be safe.

Assuming a 6 percent return rate and the $1.25 million amount from our previous example, you need to save around $218,000 across 30 years to achieve this projected retirement goal.

That equals $605 per month or $7,266 a year.

Step 2: Open a Retirement Account

Open a retirement account as soon as you've determined what you'll need to save. Stock market investments are the best method for increasing your retirement funds since they have historically provided much better yields than savings accounts.

Not all investment vehicles are ideal for retirement savings. However, the federal government has developed unique investment accounts, commonly referred to as retirement accounts, which offer certain tax benefits to encourage folks to start putting money aside for retirement.

Employer-sponsored retirement accounts, such as 401(k)s and individual retirement accounts, are the 2 main categories of retirement accounts (IRAs). Both standard and Roth account options are typically offered for both types of accounts. They both provide tax-advantaged growth for your investment capital, but you get to decide whether you would rather avoid paying income taxes now or in the future.

Below are the 2 most important/prevalent retirement accounts:

a) Employer-Sponsored Retirement Accounts

Companies provide their employees with advantages, including employer-sponsored retirement programs. The most well-known is the 401(k), but you may also be able to access 403(b), 457(b), SEP IRA, or SIMPLE IRA based on your work location/state.

With an employment retirement plan, you typically have the option to have a percentage of each pay period automatically transferred into your retirement fund.

Company-sponsored retirement plans are advantageous because they may include employer contributions or 401(k) matches, as well as the tax advantages they provide.

These are funds that your employer has put into your retirement fund on your behalf. You must pay a specific proportion of your earnings to your retirement fund to receive a 401(k) match.

Your business makes an investment equal to that proportion in return, essentially multiplying your money by two. Other than matching payments, certain employers could provide automatic contributions to your account, such as profit-sharing or safe-harbor contributions.

As for 2020 to 2022, you are permitted to make contributions to 401(k), 403(b), and 457(b) of up to $19,500 annually ($26,000 if you are 50 years of age or older).

Employee contributions are not permitted in SEP IRAs. Still, your employer may contribute an amount of up to 25 percent of your salary or, in the years 2021 and 2022, a maximum of $58,000 ($57,000) yearly.

In 2020 and 2021, you are permitted to make annual contributions to SIMPLE IRAs of up to $13,500 ($16,500 if you're 50 or older).

b) *Individual Retirement Accounts (IRAs)*

Traditional IRAs along with Roth IRAs, are your major options if you do not have any access to a work retirement account or want to drum up your retirement savings outside of it.

It would be best if you had taxable earnings for the entire year to contribute to either. Further income limitations apply to Roth IRAs. You must earn under $124,000 if you are single or $195,000 if married and filing jointly to reach the maximum Roth IRA contribution.

The IRA contribution cap for 2020 and 2021 is $5,500, or $7,000 if you are 50 or older. A Roth IRA is open to contributions from individuals with salaries up to $140,000 in 2020 ($142,000 in 2021) and couples earning up to $206,000 in 2020 ($208,000 in 2021).

Step 3: Choose Your Investments

Index funds, mutual funds, and exchange-traded funds (ETFs) are considered sound investments regarding long-term retirement savings, regardless of whether you receive a tax-advantaged retirement fund via your place of employment or start an IRA on your own.

Immediate diversification in hundreds, even thousands of equities and bonds is available through index funds. They have even consistently outpaced actively-managed mutual funds overseen by seasoned investors in the past. For most investors, a basic portfolio that consists of a bond fund and a wide market index fund, such as an S&P 500 fund, is a decent place to start.

Your asset allocation plan determines how many funds to purchase and the proportion of your balance you need to put in each fund. This strategy helps you allocate your retirement assets effectively across various investments by balancing your risk appetite with the period you have until retirement.

The performance of your retirement account doesn't need to be monitored frequently, but as you get older, you'll probably want to change the proportion of bonds, stocks, and cash in your portfolio. Your portfolio may deviate from your intended asset allocation over time.

Deliberate going for robo-advisors or target-date funds, if you desire to save for retirement in a set-it-and-forget-it, hands-off manner. These excellent solutions provide pre-mixed retirement portfolios and automatically modify your investments as you grow older and the market changes for a little cost.

Many corporate retirement programs and brokerages that offer IRAs offer target-date funds. In general, robo-advisors let you open IRAs; but certain businesses might collaborate with them to provide their staff workplace retirement accounts.

Step 4: Set Up Automatic Recurring Deposits

The majority of financial consultants advise you to establish a regular rhythm of contributions into your retirement savings, whether those accounts are in an IRA or a 401(k) through your employer.

You are probably already set if your employer offers a 401(k). If you are using an IRA to make investments, ensure your routine deposits won't exceed the allowed annual restrictions.

This stops you from being required to devote the time and effort to investing each week or month and using the money you would rather save.

The potent concept known as dollar-cost averaging may also enable you to pay less for a share, on average.

Step 5: Regularly Increase Your Retirement Savings Rate

It's okay if you can't instantly set aside 15 percent of your salary for retirement. You can start small but as early as possible to benefit from the critical role that time will play in compounding your investment returns.

Many financial consultants advise you to boost the amount you put in your retirement account by 1 percent per year until you achieve at least 15 percent of your pay to aid you in achieving your savings goals. You can also do the following to enhance your retirement savings:

- Set aside a percentage of bonuses or raises automatically. Adjust your contributions as soon as possible to deposit the additional money in your wage to your account if you receive a bonus or increase.

- Save any windfalls. If you receive a tax refund or other unanticipated windfall, consider contributing some, most, or perhaps even all of it to your IRA.

- After paying off your debt, put those payment sums toward your retirement. Don't use the money you were paying toward spending as you paid down your credit card, auto, or student debts. Simply direct your regular monthly payments toward your retirement funds.

- Keep lifestyle inflation at bay. Our propensity to spend extra whenever we have more money is known as lifestyle inflation or lifestyle creep. Try to make by with the resources you have to reduce your expenses and direct your additional money to your savings instead of moving to a bigger home or buying a new automobile once you receive a raise.

Step 6: Open an Additional Retirement Account

There are many benefits to having multiple retirement accounts, perhaps even two. If the employer-sponsored retirement plan you're on has excessively high costs or you are dissatisfied with its investment choices, you might consider opening additional retirement accounts.

If you have been diligent about saving this year, you may want to open a second retirement account if your first account's yearly contribution limitations have been reached.

Set aside an additional $6,000 for retirement, or $7,000 if you are 50 or older, and think about starting a regular or Roth IRA (of course, depending on your eligibility).

Once you've made the maximum annual IRA contributions, your account selections will now be more constrained. Consider investing a portion of your income in a SEP IRA or Solo 401(k) if you run a side business. Just keep in mind that yearly contribution restrictions apply to all accounts, even if you have multiple IRAs and 401(k)s.

And if you are a great saver and have used up all your alternatives for tax-advantaged retirement accounts, consider opening a taxable brokerage account. They are a highly valuable tool for continuing to invest for retirement, despite not having the favorable tax status of many retirement accounts.

Step 7: Keep Things in Perspective Through Good Times and Bad

The stock exchange has historically experienced average returns of around 10%. Average is the crucial word in that phrase. The stock market yardstick, the S&P 500, has occasionally increased by more than 20 percent. There have been other years when its overall performance has drastically declined.

Remember that the stock market has always recovered from periods of poor performance and continued to rise when investing for long-term objectives like retirement. Therefore, don't let the performance of your retirement portfolio, from one day to the next or even from one month or year to the next, get you too worked up.

You must consider the long picture since retirement is, at its core, a long game.

You now know what to do to start saving up for retirement. Next up, we look at something that will be very important with regard to the savings we make – compound interest and the power it yields.

Chapter 5: The Power of Compound Interest

Compound interest is when interest on your balance, either in a savings or investment account, is reinvested. This results in higher interest payments which get cumulatively higher when the money is given more time to generate interest. A wise man once said that money makes money.

Compound interest will accelerate your savings and assets' growth over time. Conversely, compound interest also increases your debt loads over time. In the same way that compound interest accelerates the growth of your savings and investments, it will also accelerate the growth of your debts.

This is why ensuring that your debt gets compounded as infrequently as possible is essential. But we'll touch on this later in the chapter.

Below, is all the information you require regarding compound interest. We'll start right at the start – by covering what it is.

What Is Compound Interest?

The *"interest that you earn on interest"* is what is known as compound interest. You don't merely earn interest on the principal balance when you use compound interest. Even your interest is compounded.

When you add the interest you have already earned back onto your principal balance, you earn compound interest, increasing your profits.

Simple math may illustrate this: if you've got $100, which generates 5% interest annually, you will have $105 when the first year is up. You will wind up with $110.25 after the 2nd year. In addition to earning $5 on your initial deposit of $100, you also made $0.25 on the interest generated on that amount.

Although 25 cents may not seem like a lot at first, it rapidly adds up. Compound interest means that even if you never add another dollar to your account, in 10 years, you will have over $162, and in 20 years, you will have approximately $340.

Assume that you've got $1,000 in your savings account, earning 5% interest annually. If you made $50 in the first year, your new balance would be $1,050. Your new amount at the end of year two would be

$1,102.50 as you'd earn 5 percent on the greater balance of $1,050 in year two, or $52.50.

Compound interest's magic allows your account balance to increase faster over time as you collect interest on progressively growing balances. A balance of $4,321.94 would result from leaving $1,000 in our hypothetical savings account for thirty years at a rate of 5% yearly interest while never making any more deposits.

Interest can be compounded or added back to your principal at varied intervals. For instance, interest may be compounded continuously, each day, each month, or even each year. Your principal balance will grow quicker the more often its interest is compounded.

In keeping with the example above, if you opened a savings account with a $1,000 amount and the interest you received was compounded daily rather than annually, you would have an overall balance of $4,481.23 at the end of 30 years. This shows that with interest being compounded more regularly, you would have made an extra $160.

How Compound Interest Works

The best way to illustrate this is to compare and contrast both simple and compound interests. This is done below:

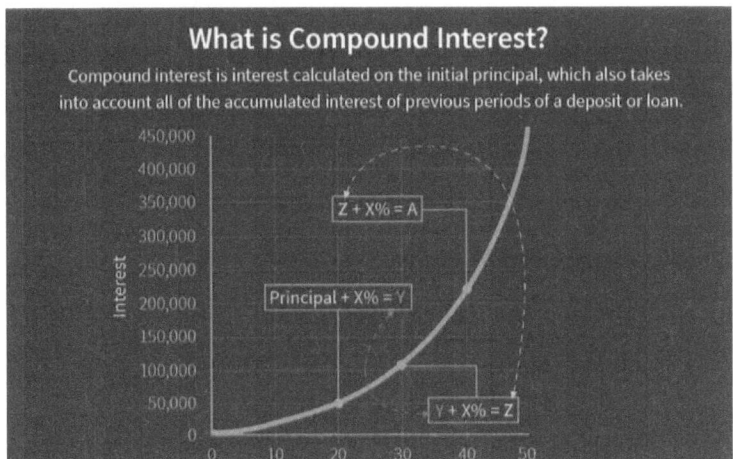

Simple Interest Vs. Compound Interest

Compound interest works in a markedly different way compared to simple interest, the latter of which is more straightforward and a lot easier to grasp. For starters, only the principal (the initial figure you deposited/invested) is used to compute simple interest. When calculating simple interest, the generated interest isn't compounded or invested back into the principle. Basically, only the principal amount is used to create interest.

When calculating simple interest, you would receive $50 annually from a $1,000 account balance earning 5% annual interest. The principle would not be increased by the amount of interest generated.

You would receive an additional $50 in year two.

The interest payable on auto loans and other short-term consumer loans is frequently calculated using simple interest. On the other hand, interest on credit card debt is usually compounded, which is why it often seems like credit card debt balloons so quickly compared to other kinds of debt.

With all the above internalized, in a perfect world, compound interest would be used to compute your investments and savings, while simple interest would be used to calculate your debts.

Understanding Compound Interest Calculations

You must internalize a few crucial components in order to understand and be able to calculate compound interest accurately. The following five elements are critical to comprehending compound interest. Each plays a unique part in the final product, and some factors might have a significant impact on your results:

1. Interest – This is the interest rate that you either earn or pay. You either earn more money or owe more money when the interest rate rises.

2. Principal amount – How much cash are you working with initially? What amount did you borrow? Even though compounding goes up over time, everything depends on the primary contribution or loan sum.

3. Periodicity/regularity of compounding – How quickly a balance rises depends on how interest is compounded: annually,

monthly, or daily. Ensure you know how regularly interest compounds before signing up for a loan or starting a savings account.

4. Duration – How long do you plan to keep an account open or repay a loan? You will either make more money or owe more if you keep savings in an account or hold onto a debt for longer.

5. Deposits and withdrawals – Do you intend to deposit money into your account regularly? How frequently will you pay back the loan? Over time, a lot will depend on how quickly you increase your principal balance or reduce your loan balance.

The Compound Interest Formula

Compound interest can be calculated in several ways. Use an online calculator to do the arithmetic for you; this is by far the easiest method, and these are free on the internet.

But occasionally, being able to view and work with the moving elements in a more "manual" format is useful. Plus, it never hurts to know the inner workings and individual elements of things,

Here's the compound interest formula:

$A = P (1 + [r / n])$ ^ nt

$A = P (1 + rt)$

A = the total money amount accumulated after a period of n years, inclusive of interest

P = the principal/initial amount (this is the initial deposit or the initial bill on your credit card)

r = the yearly interest rate (in decimal)

n = the total times your interest is compounded yearly

t = the total number of years (time) that your money will have been deposited for

It's crucial to remember that the yearly interest rate is calculated by dividing it by the total number of times it is compounded annually. Depending on the compounding frequency, you are given the average interest rate daily, monthly, or annually.

Here's an example of how that works in terms of numbers:

Assume you deposit $5,000 into your savings account that offers 5% interest. The account will be compounded every month for ten years.

You know of P ($5,000), r (.05), n (12), and t in this case (10). Let's now include those in the formula for compound interest.

$A = P (1 + [r / n]) \wedge nt$

$A = 5,000 (1 + [.05 / 12]) \wedge (12 * 10)$

$A = 5,000 (1.00417) \wedge (120)$

$A = 5,000 (1.64767)$

$A = 8,238.35$

You would have roughly $8,238 in your account after ten years. That includes your $3,238 interest on top of the $5,000 initial deposit.

It becomes more difficult if you plan on adding more money deposits to your account. Microsoft Excel is the best option to accurately calculate your compounded interest, albeit you can still figure this out without it.

Let us look at computing compound interest using MS Excel in the instance that you keep adding to your savings and having compound interest work its magic on your nest egg:

Compound Interest Formula Excel

You can compute compound interest using Microsoft Excel by using the Future Value (FV) function:

= FV (rate, nper, pmt, [pv], [type])

FV = This represents the future value

rate = the rate of interest per period

nper = the total number of times the interest is computed

pmt = the additional monies that you add each period

pv = This means the **present value**, or the primary deposit. If you leave this out, it is tallied as 0.

type = This represents either the number 0 or 1. 0 represents any payments are due at the end of the period, while 1 means payments are due at the start. If you omit this, it's assumed to be 0.

If you omit the pmt variable, you will get a similar result as the 1st equation. To continue with our example above; here is what would unfold if you decided to add an extra $100 each month to the primary $5,000 deposit:

= FV (0.05/12,10*12,100,5000,0)

After ten years, at an interest rate of 5%, you would have about $23,763.

If you do not fancy doing the math yourself, then an online compound interest calculator will do all the heavy lifting for you.

Let's now compare this with having simple interest working on your savings:

Simple Interest Formula

You will use a simplified compound interest formula version to calculate simple interest:

A = P (1 + rt)

A = the total money amount accumulated after a period of n years, inclusive of interest

P = the principal/initial amount (this is the initial deposit or the initial bill on your credit card)

r = the annual interest rate (as a decimal)

t = the total number of years (time) that your money amount will have been deposited for

If our hypothetical $5,000 only earns simple interest; here is how we'd go about calculating it:

A = P (1 + rt)

A = 5,000 (1 + [.05 * 10])

A = 5,000 (1 + .5)

A = 5,000 (1.5)

A = 7,500

After 10 years, with a simple interest rate of 5%; you'd have $7,500, which is over $700 less compared to a scenario where your money had been compounded monthly.

Examples of Compound Interest

Depending if you are borrowing money or saving for retirement, compound interest will either aid you or cost you big. The idea is to have it aid you big and help accelerate the growth of your retirement account, further propping up your retirement plan and helping you retire comfortably.

Below are examples where compound interest works its magic:

1. Accounts for savings, checking, and deposit certificates (CDs)

The interest will be credited to your savings account and promptly directed to your balance when you deposit funds into a bank account that accrues interest, such as your retirement savings account. As a result, your balance will grow steadily.

2. Investment accounts and 401(k) accounts

Compounding is also a feature of your 401(k) and investment account earnings. Since stock gains are computed daily based on the previous day's performance, they compound daily throughout business hours. You could aid your balance to grow even quicker if you reinvested your dividends and made consistent deposits.

3. Mortgages, personal loans, and student loans

When you borrow money, compound interest actively works against you. If you borrow money and don't pay it back or are infrequent in making payments, interest will be charged on top of the interest accrued, leading to increasingly more significant financial hits.

Basically, the interest costs are "capitalized," or allocated to your original loan sum, if you do not pay them within the time frame specified in your loan agreement.

Future interest is then charged on the new, increased loan balance. Use an online student loan calculator to determine how much extra payments will cost you and how much interest will accrue; there are plenty of these on the internet, and they are entirely free to use.

4. Credit cards

Your credit card will charge interest on the outstanding debt each month. Your balance will remain unchanged if you do not add any further purchases to your card and make the monthly interest payment.

But if you do not make enough payments to meet the increased interest for the month, it will be added to the balance on your credit card. The interest for the subsequent month is then computed using the larger sum. This may cause your balance to decline rapidly over time.

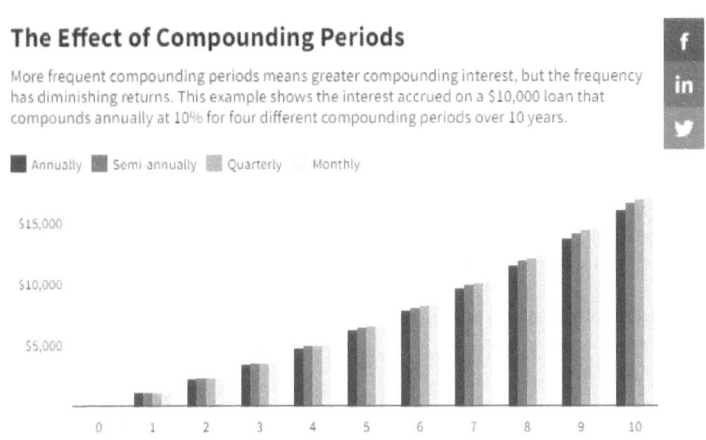

Harnessing the Power of Compound Interest by Starting to Save Early

Young people either make a habit of forgetting to make retirement savings or simply ignore it. Because for most, the future looks so far away to folks in their twenties that other expenses seem more pressing.

Compound interest, however, will be an absolute game-changer if you start to harness it right in this instance, as it allows you to save much more quickly, with smaller amounts in savings, than you would later in life by saving larger sums of money.

Below, is an illustration of its impact if you start saving as early as possible:

Suppose you invest in the market in your 20s at a steady investment clip of $100 per month. Then, suppose that throughout 40 years you generate a net positive return of about 1 percent every month (12 percent annually). Now, imagine you have an identical twin, who's the same age, and they start investing 30 years from now. Your tardy brother/sister then makes $1,000 monthly investments for ten years, averaging the same favorable return.

Your twin will have amassed roughly $230,000 in savings when you reach your 40-year mark for saving, while you'll have a little over $1.17 million. Your portfolio grows dramatically, in this case by a factor of approximately more than 5, even though they have been investing ten times as much as you have (and even considerably more toward the end). This will all be owed to the magic of compound interest.

Using an employer-sponsored retirement fund, such as the 401(k) or 403(b), or starting a private retirement account (IRA), follows pretty much the same logic. Start directing funds into it, no matter how small the amounts are, and be consistent while you are in your 20s (if you are). You'll be happy that you did when your nest egg grows exponentially by the time your retirement years roll in sight.

Here are a couple more scenarios to further illustrate the point:

Scenario #2

Ryan gave the following illustration of compound interest: Assume Sarah, 20 years old, invested $1,000 today. She could see a 32-fold return on her investment if she did not touch it right up until she reached 70 and retired, leaving her with almost $32,000. (Based on the historical, long-term U.S. large-cap equities returns, Ryan's claim of a 7.2 percent growth rate is acceptable.)

But what if Sarah held off investing her $1,000 until retirement for another ten years until she was 30? In such a scenario, she would only receive $16,000, or half of what was previously stated. What if Sarah waited even longer until she was 40? That would reduce the sum she would have left by another half to about $8,000.

The real kicker — or "where it really gets magical," says Ryan — is that Sarah would have $465,000 at age 70 if she invested that $1,000 at 20 years of age and made monthly contributions of $83 (or about $1,000) until retirement.

If she had done the same thing but started later, at age 30, she would have had around $225,000; at age 40, she would have had about $105,000.

Retirement Planning

Scenario #3

Let's look at two different folks who are investing and saving for their retirement in another example of interest compounding.

Let's imagine that over 20 years, Tom, 45, and Charlotte, 25, both save $30,000 apiece (they each save $1,000 each year for the first 10 years, then $2,000 per year for the next 10 years.) We'll assume that they make their annual contributions at year's end and that there is a 6 percent yearly return.

In this case, Tom starts saving at age 45 and ceases at age 64, while Charlotte begins saving at 25 and ceases at age 44. Charlotte will have an extra $110,000 in her nest fund than Tom when he turns 65, even though they both saved the same amount and received the same rate of return. Charlotte gets $160,300 in total, while Tom receives $49,970.

Unlike Tom's money, which can grow up to 20 years, Charlotte's money can expand by up to 40 years because of the magic of compounding. Tom would have to accumulate upwards of thrice as much as Charlotte to have a comparably sized nest egg when he gets to 65 because he starts saving later.

The kicker: Charlotte would have roughly $243,000 if she continued to save until age 65 instead of stopping at 44.

You want to allow yourself as much time as you can with compound interest, Ryan explains. "The sooner you begin investing and saving for retirement (or for any other objective, really), the more time you will have to benefit from compounding. It's too nice to pass up; in a way, it's free money.

Pros and Cons of Compounding

Despite the apocryphal story of Albert Einstein referring to it as the 8th world wonder and man's greatest creation ever, compounding can (and usually will) actively work against borrowers who have debts with extremely high-interest rates, e.g., credit card debt.

A $20,000 credit card load held at a monthly compounded interest rate of 20 percent would accrue a total compounded interest of $4,390 over a year, or around $365 each month.

On the plus side, compounding can help you with your investments and be a significant contributor to wealth accumulation. Exponential monetary growth from compound interest also helps to counter wealth-corroding factors like rising living costs, inflation, and declining purchasing power.

One of the simplest and best ways for saving folks and investors to gain from compound interest is through mutual funds. More of the fund's shares will be bought when dividends from a mutual fund are picked to be reinvested. The cycle of buying more shares will keep the fund investment growing in value as more compounded interest is accumulated over time.

Consider an investment in a mutual fund that you open with, say, $5,000 and then add $2,400 every year. The investment will be worth $798,500 after 30 years at an average yearly return of 12%. Compound interest will be the prime difference between the initial investment's cash contribution and its real future worth.

Compound interest will be $722,550 in this case, which is the future total after committing $77,000; or a collective contribution of merely $200 each month over a period of 30 years.

Keep in mind that compound interest profits are taxable unless they are kept in tax-sheltered accounts. It is typically taxed at the regular rate determined by your particular tax bracket, and your balance may decrease if those investments in your portfolio drop in value.

When investing, the compounding power is efficiently being used by an investor who goes for a DRIP (dividend reinvestment plan) in a brokerage account.

When purchasing a zero-coupon bond, you can also benefit from compound interest. As per the original provisions of the bond issue, conventional bond issues offer investors periodic interest payments. Since these deposits are made to the investor through checks, the interest doesn't compound.

Investors don't get interest payments from zero-coupon bonds. Instead, this kind of bond is bought below its initial value and increases in value over time. Zero-coupon bond benefactors employ compound interest to raise the bond's value until it arrives at its total value at maturity.

When paying back loans, compounding can also be advantageous. Your amortization term will be shortened, and you'll save a significant interest if you pay half of your loan/mortgage payment twice a month instead of the entire amount once a month.

Is it possible for Compound Interest Make You Rich?

Yes. Perhaps the most powerful tool for generating money ever invented is compound interest. Compound interest has been utilized to create cash by bankers, traders, and other entrepreneurs for, quite literally, thousands upon thousands of years, as per the archives. For instance, ancient Babylon employed clay tablets over 4,000 years ago to teach students the math of compounded interest.

The business method Warren Buffett used to become one of the wealthiest persons in the world today entailed diligently and slowly compounding investment returns over extended periods of time. Compound interest will probably continue to be used by humans to create wealth in some capacity for the conceivable future.

Making Compound Interest Work for You

Here are several directives that will help make compound interest work for you:

1. Plan out your savings/investment schedule and give yourself ample time

The power that sheer time carries is just about everything when it comes to compound interest. The longer you allow your money to sit and grow, the more time it does.

For this reason, it's crucial to begin saving for your retirement as soon as feasible to help your retirement savings grow in size.

2. Debt should be paid off quickly

Whether you borrow money through credit cards, school loans, or other means, compound interest will actively work against you. Over time, you will owe less if you can pay things down more quickly.

3. Examine APYs

In comparison to the annual percentage rate, APR, the annual percentage yield, APY, will offer you a clearer understanding of the interest you'll earn or be paid. This is because the APY considers compounding, whereas the APR only considers the simple interest rate.

4. Check the compounding rate

You'll make more money if your retirement savings account regularly compounds interest. Your savings and investment assets should compound as often as practicable, while your debts should compound as infrequently as possible.

The Bottom Line

Your savings, as well as retirement potential, can be greatly increased by compounding through compound interest. Successful compounding enables you to achieve your goals with less of your personal money.

Compounding can, however, also be used against you, as when high-interest credit card debt accumulates over time.

Therefore, compounding is a strong incentive to pay off debt as quickly as possible and to start saving and investing money early.

Chapter 6: Accounts You Can Use to Invest In Retirement

Retirement, especially for those of us still in our 30s – even 40s – may seem so far off in the future that it may not appear overbearingly essential to think about at the moment. However, you can argue that you can never start too early because the earlier you get started, the sooner you will be able to cease worrying about retiring with nothing to fall back on and focus on living your life to the fullest.

According to a 2020 Statista survey, 41% of US citizens have less than $100,000 saved up for retirement. This is quite dangerous, and future generations are, by default, plunged into a vulnerable position, especially since they won't have enough money to finance their post-work lifestyles due to the shrinking support provided by pensions and Social Security.

It's crucial to remember that there is no one clear-cut, fail-proof strategy for saving for retirement. But with the historically low rates of interest and increasing inflation, keeping your money stewing in a savings account is probably not going to make a difference, or at least the kind of difference you would like. You need to invest to achieve your retirement goals and live a worry-free life when retired.

You can increase your money through the accounts listed below, and you will also be able to get specific tax benefits to boot.

So, which are these accounts? Well, before we look at them, let's first look at key plan benefits you should consider before making your move:

Key Plan Benefits to Consider

Nearly all retirement plans provide tax benefits, whether accessible upfront, during saving, or while you are taking withdrawals. For instance, traditional 401(k) contributions are made with pre-tax money, significantly lowering your taxable income. Contrarily, Roth 401(k) plans allow for tax-free withdrawals even when financed with after-tax funds.

Some retirement savings plans, like 401(k) or 403(b) plans, also feature stipulated matching contributions from your employer, while others do not. If your employer matches your contributions, choose the 401(k) plan rather than an individual retirement account (IRA) — or, if you are in a position to, choose both. We'll look at this more in this chapter.

Make sure you're taking full advantage of the employer match if you were automatically enrolled in your employer's 401(k) plan. These matches will go a long way decades later when you're retired.

Additionally, consider increasing your yearly contribution because too many plans will start you off at a pitiful deferral amount that is insufficient to provide true retirement security, even with compounding working its magic.

According to Vanguard, the typical savings deferral rate for 401(k) plans that provide automatic enrolment is just 3%. However, T. Rowe Price, a world-renowned global investment management firm, advises that you "seek to save, at minimum, 15% of your salary each year for retirement."

You have a variety of retirement savings options if you work for yourself. You can invest in a Roth IRA or regular IRA, subject to a specific income threshold, with lesser yearly funding limits than most other plans – in addition to the rest of the programs covered below for salaried employees and business owners. Additionally, you have several more choices that not everyone has, such as the SIMPLE IRA, SEP IRA, and the solo 401(k).

Here are the accounts you may want to consider:

The Best Retirement Plans to Consider In November 2022 And Beyond

1. Defined contribution plans

Defined contribution plans, also called DC plans, which include 401(k)s, have taken over the retirement marketplace since their inception in the early 80s. According to a recently conducted research study by insurance broker Willis Towers Watson, one of the top insurance companies in America, approximately 86% of Fortune 500 businesses offered only DC plans by 2019, eschewing traditional pensions altogether. This speaks a lot about the massive popularity of these plans.

The 403(b) plan, which is also included in the DC plan umbrella and covered in this chapter, is available to public school employees and some tax-exempt organizations. In comparison, the 457(b) plan, which we will also cover, is most frequently offered to local and state government staff.

The 401(k) plan is by some distance the most overall DC plan among employers, regardless of size. As of 2022, each plan's employee contribution cap is set at $20,500 ($27,000 for employees over 50). Many DC plans provide a Roth option, for example, the Roth 401(k), in which you make contributions with after-tax money but can withdraw the funds tax-free when you retire.

If you anticipate that your individual tax rate will be greater after you retire than it is now, the Roth option makes all the sense in the world and should be a priority.

Below are the varied kinds of DC plans:

a) 401(k) plans

The 401(k) plan, a tax-advantaged plan, gives you a defined, well-set-up way to save money for retirement. With a standard 401(k), an employee makes contributions to the plan out of pre-tax income, which means that the contributions are not taxable.

These contributions can grow tax-free in your 401(k) plan until they are withdrawn during retirement. Although withdrawals made before age 59½ could be subject to taxation and added penalties, distributions at retirement result in a taxable gain.

Employees can contribute after-tax money to a Roth 401(k), and the gains generated will not be taxed as long as you withdraw them after reaching 59½ years old. Making withdrawals before you reach this age will attract additional penalties and fees.

Pros: A 401(k) plan will simplify saving for your retirement since you can automate investments and withdrawals from your paycheck. You are not required to pay tax on your gains and profits until you take out your money, and your funds can be quickly and efficiently channeled and invested in various high-return investments like equities. Additionally, many employers tend to match 401(k) contributions, furnishing your retirement plan with extra money.

Cons: The possibility of incurring fees while using your saved-up funds for an emergency is a major drawback of 401(k) plans. There is also no assurance that your employer's plan will permit you to borrow against your money for permissible purposes, even though this is legally allowed under many plans.

You may also not be able to channel and invest your money in what you want to since your investments are restricted to the funds offered in your employer's 401(k) program.

What this plan means to you: Setting up a 401(k) plan is hands down one of the finest methods to save up for retirement, and you will be able to save even more quickly if your company offers a bonus "match."

b) 403(b) plans

The 403(b) plan is quite similar to a 401(k), except it is provided by institutions, including public schools, nonprofit organizations, and some religious institutions - mostly churches. The funds in the plan will grow completely tax-free until you reach retirement.

Since you, the employee, will be contributing pre-tax money to it, your contributions are not regarded as taxable income, hence will have no taxes slapped onto them. Withdrawals are considered regular income upon retirement, and any distributions made before the age of 59½ can result in additional penalties and taxes.

With a Roth 403(b), you can make after-tax contributions and tax-free withdrawals in retirement, as is the case with a Roth 401(k).

Pros: A 403(b) is a popular and efficient way to save up for retirement. You can arrange for your funds to be routinely drawn from your salary, which will put you in a position to increase your savings.

You also aren't required to pay any taxes on the investment income until you take it out. You can channel the funds to various investments, such as annuity packages (which we will look at later) or high-return assets like stock funds.

If you put money down in a 403(b), your employer may also provide a matching contribution, making it possible for you to save even more.

Cons: Similar to the 401(k), unless you do have a legitimate emergency, it will very likely prove to be very, very challenging to access the funds in a 403(b) plan. And even though you could still be able to borrow from your 403(b) plan without an emergency (again, this will be really difficult, albeit not impossible), doing so could result in additional fees and taxes.

Another drawback is that since your investment options are constrained to the plan's investment alternatives, you might not be in a position to go for the investment options of your choice.

What this plan will mean to you: This plan is one of the very best ways for you, as an employee, to save up for retirement, especially if your employer is inclined to match your contributions.

c) 457(b) plans

The 457(b) plan is only available to staff of state, local, and a few tax-exempt institutions. So, it isn't an option for a lot of folks. Nevertheless, we need to cover it as there is every chance it is an option for you or a loved one who works in a state or local institution.

You can contribute to this tax-advantaged plan following the pre-tax earnings model, which means these contributions will be tax-exempt. The 457(b) permits for tax-free growth of contributions up until retirement; however, once you withdraw the funds, Uncle Sam swoops in.

Pros: Owing to its tax benefits, the 457(b) plan is a very advantageous plan for retirement savings. The plan also provides older employees with some unique catch-up savings features that other retirement plans do not. And since the 457(b) is advantageously regarded as a supplementary savings plan, albeit it 100% functions as a full-fledged savings plan, withdrawals made before the age 59½ will not be subjected to the compulsory 10% penalty that applies to 403(b) plans as well as most other plans. This latter one, especially, is a massive perk.

Cons: Seeing as the standard 457(b) plan is not inclusive of an employer match, it is significantly less appealing than a 401(k), all things considered. Additionally, while the 10% penalty stipulation does not apply for premature withdrawals, taking an emergency withdrawal from your 457(b) plan is much more difficult than in a 401(k).

What this plan will mean to you: While a 457(b) plan has several benefits over other defined contribution plans, it also has significant disadvantages, such as those we outlined above.

The 457(b) is a solid choice for retired public officials who may suffer from physical impairment and need to access their money early because it allows withdrawals before the standard retirement age of 59½ without a penalty. Nevertheless, as we pointed out – accessing these funds early is quite the task.

2. IRA plans

The U.S. government developed the IRA set up as a useful retirement plan to further aid employees with their retirement savings and ensure as many of them enjoyed worry-free retirement as possible. As of this year, 2022, folks can deposit up to $6,000 into an account, while employees over 50 can deposit up to $7,000.

Traditional IRAs, SIMPLE IRAs, SEP IRAs, Roth IRAs, Rollover IRAs, and Spousal IRAs are just a few of the different types of IRAs available.

Here are the descriptions of each one of these and how they vary from one another:

a) Traditional IRA

You can take advantage of significant tax savings through a traditional IRA as you save up for retirement. Anyone who receives compensation for employment can make pre-tax contributions to the plan, meaning that any contributions made are not considered income.

Until the account holder withdraws them upon retirement, when they become taxable, the IRA permits these contribution amounts to grow tax-free. Early withdrawals might subject you to extra taxes and fines.

Pros: Due to its tremendous tax advantages and almost-limitless investment options, including stocks, bonds, CDs, real estate, and other assets, a traditional IRA is a particularly popular vehicle for retirement investing. The fact that you will not pay any taxes until you take the funds out at retirement is possibly the most significant advantage of this plan.

Cons: It might be expensive to withdraw funds from a traditional IRA if you need them for an emergency due to the taxes and extra penalties that get slapped on for premature withdrawals.

Additionally, an IRA mandates that you personally invest the funds, whether in a bank, equities, bonds, or whatever else. Even if all you do is ask an advisor to invest the money, you will still need to pick where and how you will do it, something that may not be of much interest to you.

What this plan will mean to you: Traditional IRAs are among the greatest retirement plans available. However, a 401(k) plan with a matching contribution is quite honestly superior and should be prioritized over this one.

And although the tax deductibility concerning contributions is lost at higher levels of income, a traditional IRA is still very much a solid option if your workplace does not provide a defined contribution plan for its employees.

b) Roth IRA

A Roth IRA, a more recent variation than a standard IRA, provides significant tax advantages. Contributions to your Roth IRA will be made with after-tax funds, which means that the funds entering the account have already been taxed. In return, you will not be required to pay taxes on any contributions withdrawn from the account once you hit retirement.

Pros: The Roth IRA has several benefits, one of which is the unique option to defer taxes on any withdrawals made from the account while in retirement, beginning at age 59 ½ or later. The Roth IRA also offers a great deal of freedom because you can frequently withdraw contributions instead of earnings at any time without paying taxes or incurring penalties. Owing to this unique flexibility, this plan is a fantastic retirement option.

Cons: You will have complete control over your investments in a Roth IRA, just like with a standard IRA. You must therefore determine how you will invest your money or get someone to do it for you for a fee (we will look at this in a separate chapter). This will undoubtedly be time-intensive, if not money-intensive.

And although there is a back-door approach to deposit money as far as the Roth IRA is concerned, there are income restrictions on contributions, with the cap set at $6,000.

What it will mean to you: Due to the significant tax benefits and unique flexibility, a Roth IRA is an excellent option if you want to grow your retirement money while avoiding additional taxation.

c) Spousal IRA

Even though IRAs are typically only available to employees with earned income, the spousal IRA allows an employee's spouse to finance an IRA as well. The spousal IRA may be either a regular or a Roth IRA; however, the working spouse's take-home pay must equal or exceed any contributions to any IRA.

Pros: The spousal IRA's main benefit is that it enables non-working spouses to benefit from all of an IRA's features, whether in the standard/traditional or Roth versions.

Cons: A spousal IRA doesn't have any unique drawbacks, but like any IRA, you'll need to decide how you will invest the funds or pay someone to do it for you. Either way, you will likely have to spend time or money on this.

What it will mean to you: The spousal IRA enables you to manage and finance your spouse or partner's retirement plan without, as would typically be the case, requiring your spouse to hold a job. This may allow your spouse to look after other family requirements or stay home.

d) SEP IRA

The SEP IRA is specifically designed for owners of small businesses and their staff. The only contributor to this retirement plan is your employer, and all contributions are made directly into each employee's SEP IRA instead of a trust fund. Those who are self-employed can also open a SEP IRA.

For self-employed people, determining contribution caps is obviously less straightforward because of apparent reasons. The 2022 contribution cap is set at either 25% of the annual salary or $61,000, whichever is smaller. Payments can be issued at the employer's discretion, making this plan comparable to a typical profit-sharing plan.

Pros: Benefits include a free retirement account for employees. The larger contribution limits make them far more appealing to self-employed people than a traditional IRA.

Cons: The amount you will accrue under this plan as an employee is uncertain because it isn't based on a specific figure but rather on the small business owner's earnings for the year.

Furthermore, it is easier to access the funds. Although this may be viewed as more of a pro than a con, some will tell you it is mostly negative because it is much easier to deplete your funds before you even reach retirement.

What it will mean to you: You will be responsible for choosing your investments, or you'll have to pay someone to do it. You'll also probably have to fork out a 10 percent penalty if you withdraw the funds before you reach age 59½, in addition to income tax, since these contributions are not considered tax-exempt. And seeing as it is a lot easier to access your funds, you need to exercise a lot of self-control to not give in to the need for early account access.

The Roth IRA plan is widely considered the best plan of them all, IRA or otherwise. Is this true?

Well, Dennis J. Farley, a young man from Louisiana, had the same question. His question was, "I am 25 and planning on opening a Roth IRA. Is investing in a Roth IRA worth it?"

Here's what Barry Gysbers, a 45-year-old Manhattan resident with a Roth account, had to say in his answer to Dennis:

"The reason why you do not know the answer to this question is because no one wants you to realize one of the most fundamental truths about saving and investing for retirement.

Let's examine the data.

Uncle Sam gives you a deal. Either you make a regular contribution to Social Security for the entirety of your working career and live on dog food when you eventually retire, or you become wealthy and keep all your money.

In fact, you may become soo wealthy that you no longer give a damn about the fact that you'll never receive the entirety of your Social Security contributions. Which deal do you choose?"

"A Roth IRA is purportedly an Individual Retirement Arrangement. Ooooh! Super Scary! Retirement! Old folks! Surely an eternity away, no? Can't touch my money for millenniums, perhaps even longer, right? At age 20, you would have to live THREE lifetimes before you get to spend your money, so this really isn't an exaggeration! Think again.

With a Roth IRA, there are never any penalties or taxes due when you withdraw your first contributions, regardless of how foolish the reason may be.

Now, I don't advise doing this. In fact, I'd rather have my right arm amputated than withdraw even a penny from my Roth IRA, but the point here is you have the option to do it. If you were in a dire financial situation and needed the money, you could access it without triggering taxes.

Then, all of your profits increase tax-free. So how many opportunities can you uncover when you can grow ALL your profits tax-free?

The profits from your Roth IRA can even be withdrawn tax-free once you reach the age of 59.5; however, as I've previously stated, I'd have my right arm amputated than withdraw even a penny from my Roth IRA."

Barry Gysbers continues, "So, what investment options are available if you DO NOT use a Roth IRA account?"

"So long as it's legal, you can purchase or sell anything. However, you pay your highest marginal tax rate on company profits, dividends, and interest, 35 percent on profits from the sale of gold and silver, and 20 percent on capital gains from investments held for a year or longer.

The bottom line remains the same even if none have the current number tagged to them any longer because the numbers fluctuate with the weather. Generally speaking, you must pay taxes on all your gains as you go, lowering the degree by which you can increase those profits by the same income taxes.

Additionally, these income taxes are **ALWAYS GREATER THAN THE 10 PERCENT ANNUAL WITHDRAWAL "PENALTY."** Earned income is subjected to more than 15 percent FICA (Social Security) and any income taxes, which, for most people who pay income taxes, reduces income by **at least 30 percent."**

"What can be purchased using a Roth IRA, you ask? Almost similar things were mentioned – except for three: collectibles, which are not always profitable; viaticals (insurance), which never generate good returns; and anything that you or your family members already own or have ever owned.

This means that you can choose from the rest of the world's products. It's akin to not being able to have sex with your cousin. It isn't a terribly limiting choice loss. You can very easily and quickly move past it. Simply choose activities that are legal and avoid breaking the law. Also, never ever USE anything and everything you purchase with a Roth IRA. I know, stupid, stupid law, but if you use, consume, eat, or spend just one night at whatever your Roth IRA helped you purchase, they will tax you dearly – or a retirement account of any other kind."

Mull over this. He makes some powerful points.

3. Solo 401(k) plan

The Solo 401(k) plan, sometimes called a Solo-k, Uni-k, or One-participant k is intended for business owners and their spouses.

The business owner serves as both the employee and the employer by allowing elective deferrals that can rise to $20,500 and non-elective contributions that can rise to 25% of pay for total yearly contributions for organizations of $61,000 (excluding catch-up payments).

Pros: A solo IRA is preferable to a SIMPLE IRA if you do not have other employees except you and your spouse, as you can contribute even more to it. Setting up and terminating the SEP is also considerably simpler.

And with a Solo-k, you can actually set it up as a Roth, reaping further benefits such as not having to pay taxes on contributions and gains, something that you will not be able to do with a SEP.

Cons: It requires a little more work to set up, and if your assets surpass $250,000, you must submit a Form 5500-SE yearly report.

What it will mean to you: This plan will not work if you intend to grow your company and hire lots of personnel. As soon as you bring on new employees, the IRS requires that, if they are eligible, they be part of the plan and that non-discrimination testing be performed regularly on the plan. Additionally, the single 401(k) compares favorably to the remarkably popular SEP IRA.

The different accounts outlined here beg the question – just how many accounts can I have? We'll answer this question by looking at what several ordinary, non-celebrity folks that you can perhaps relate to have to say about this:

How Many Retirement Accounts Can I Have?

1. Gerald McGowan says:

How many can you have? I had 4.

- An employer-paid pension program.

- I started an IRA in the 1970s.

- A 401(k) plan from my work, to which they and I both contributed.

Before retiring, I contributed to Social Security for forty years, and it took me over fifty years to receive any benefits. My wife also has Social Security and an IRA with her numerous retirement plans from her various employment.

Therefore, we presently gather data from six sources. Each is small, but together they make it possible for us to live comfortably.

"Plan and save," if there ever was a true catchphrase. Please don't put it off because you want, say, to go on a great vacation; start early. Keep it for the inevitable event known as "retirement." I've been on a 23-year vacation so far and loving it.

2. **Christopher Richards, who describes himself as semi-retired, says:**

Theoretically, you can have as many in the USA. Yes, I'm happy I made my intentions when I was 16, 20, and 35. If I had not, I'd be in serious trouble right now.

While one of my strategies has failed (yet another reason to have multiple plans), at least I've received partial compensation, so my loss is not total. At least three additional plans are running concurrently.

I've had a lot of trouble saving money for retirement pensions because of things that happened 20 years ago, but I still managed to contribute to one of them, at the very least. Therefore, I now have only 4 live policies.

I would advise against having too many because of the inflation rate and the fees associated with maintaining the funds. You should keep your overall number of funds low to prevent the assets from being wiped out.

3. **Brett Marks, a former retired attorney, says:**

Here in the US, the answer is yes; you can have multiple.

A husband and wife both with jobs could, for instance, have the following:

- 2 IRAs, one of which may be a Roth

- 2 401k's (or state equivalents)

- Pensions from Health Savings Accounts 2 (possibly more)

- 2 streams of Social Security

Additionally, this pair could invest additional funds for retirement in life insurance, annuities, and non-retirement brokerage accounts.

The vast majority of individuals will only have a small subset of the above accounts; however, anyone can have a number of these accounts.

Here is my own real-life example:

- Husband - Social Security, standard IRA, a Rollover IRA (a former 401k), a Roth IRA (a conversion from a Rollover IRA), a pension, and an annuity.

- Wife - Traditional IRA, Social Security, pension, and annuity

- Joint - Brokerage accounts that provide significant income and tax-free interest throughout retirement

These are eleven distinct accounts or sources of revenue. We have more than enough money in these accounts to cover our expenses; therefore, we are actively reinvesting to increase our investment wealth.

With all the information you have from this chapter, you can choose your ideal plan. But take your time and do as much research as you can before making an outright choice. Next up, we examine a subject that we've already touched on earlier – social security – and how you can best take advantage of it to the maximum.

Chapter 7: How to Take Advantage of Social Security as Part of Your Retirement Plan

We covered social security in great depth in the introductory chapter and the first two chapters of this guide. We covered why the deductions are made from your paycheck as you work, how social security works, the earliest you can begin collecting these payments (62 years), why you shouldn't have these payments as your main retirement finances crutch, and a whole host of other things.

As such, we will not cover all of this again as that would be redundant since we already did a comprehensive job helping you understand what it is and how it works.

Since you understand social security and how it does (and does not) work, this chapter will primarily focus on how you can best take advantage of it and how you can help maximize these payments.

Let's get started:

Employees contribute to the social security fund via payroll taxes over what is, pretty much, a lifetime of work. You're more than familiar with this, given that these payments are taken out of your paycheck. So why not make the most of your benefits?

A portion of your salary regularly goes toward social security, so you may as well get as much of it back as possible when the time comes. This chapter shows you how you can boost your social security benefits.

You can begin receiving your Social Security retirement payments as soon as at 62. Once you hit full retirement age, you can then be qualified for the whole scope of social security benefits. The benefit amount will be more if you wait until you are 70 years old before claiming your benefits. However, waiting longer than 70 years of age will not offer you any extra advantages, as these get capped at 70. We'll look at this later in this chapter.

It is essential to know that your benefits will be cut by a small percentage for every month that you commence receiving benefits before you reach full retirement age.

Use the chart below and choose your birth year to determine how much your benefits will decrease if you start getting benefits from the age of 62 all the way up to the full retirement age. This example is based on an assumed $1,000 monthly pension at full retirement age.

Full Retirement and Age 62 Benefit by Year of Birth

Year of Birth [1]	Full (normal) Retirement Age	Months between age 62 and full retirement age [2]	At Age 62 [3]		A $500 spouse benefit would reduce
			A $1000 retirement benefit would be reduced to	The retirement benefit is reduced by [4]	
1943-1954	66	48	$750	25.00%	$350
1955	66 and 2 months	50	$741	25.83%	$345
1956	66 and 4 months	52	$733	26.67%	$341
1957	66 and 6 months	54	$725	27.50%	$337
1958	66 and 8 months	56	$716	28.33%	$333
1959	66 and 10 months	58	$708	29.17%	$329
1960 and later	67	60	$700	30.00%	$325

Here are some directives that will help you use this chart:

1) You should refer to the previous year if your birthday is on January 1.

2) If your birthday falls on the first of the month, your benefit (and full retirement age) will be calculated as if it fell in the previous month. Say if your birthday is on January 1, your benefit (in addition to your full retirement age) will be computed as if your birthday is in December.

3) You must be 62 years old to qualify for benefits for the entire month (this is why you refer to the previous month if your birthday is on the 1st of the month).

4) Percentages are rounded, and as such, they are not exact, and you shouldn't take them as such.

5) The spouse's benefit can go up to 50% of what the employee would get at full retirement age. The spouse's percentage discount should be applied after the automatic 50% reduction. Again, owing to rounding, the percentages are approximate and not exact.

Before You Make a Decision to Withdraw Retirement Funds

The decision to get your benefits before reaching full retirement age has benefits and drawbacks. You can gain from collecting benefits for longer if you're a financially savvy person who knows what to invest in and when.

But let's be honest here; most of us are not financial gurus of this mold. Most of us are not even interested in the intricacies of investment. The obvious drawback here is that your benefit amount will be scaled back. Each individual's situation will be different.

However, it is vital to remember:

A) You will be eligible to deferred retirement credits, which would boost your monthly income if you wait to collect your benefits until after reaching full retirement age.

B) There are additional factors to consider when deciding when to start receiving retirement benefits.

C) You should still enroll for Medicare coverage within 3 months of turning 65, even if you postpone receiving them until later in life. Your Medicare medical insurance (Part B) and prescription drug coverage (Part D) could become more expensive if you wait longer.

You can take actions that will significantly increase your ability to receive the most out of your Social Security retirement payments.

Strategies to Boost Your Benefits

The following strategies, some of which have qualifying restrictions, can be either used singly or combined:

1. Work for 35 Years

You may be eligible for Social Security payments after working for as little as ten years. You can also start receiving your social security benefits as early as 62 or as late as 70. The rounded-off average of your thirty-five highest-earning years determines how much you will receive in benefits. Fewer years of employment result in those zeros being averaged in.

Since your benefit is calculated based on your strongest earning years, it increases as your income does. But there are limits. The benefits for 2023 are capped at $2,572 for retirees who are 62 years old, $3,506 for those who are 66 years old and older, and $4,555 for folks who are 70 years old.

2. Wait Until at Least Full Retirement Age

You can retire from work as early as 62 and claim Social Security payments, as shown by the peak levels above, but the problem with this is your benefits will be slashed by 25% to 30%. The full retirement age is 66 for those born after 1942, with two months being added for every year after 1954. It is age 67 for people born in 1960 and later.

As such, to receive the maximum amount you are qualified for, it is advisable to hold off on collecting until you reach full retirement age. You can even wait longer and qualify for deferred retirement credits, thereby raising your monthly payment, but only go this route if it makes sense for your particular scenario.

Important note: You will receive an additional 8% annually if you wait to begin receiving benefits until you are 70 rather than 62. The percentage bumps end at 70, meaning there are no extra benefits if you wait past 70.

3. Sign Up for Spousal Benefits

Married people with low-earned incomes may be eligible for spousal benefits equal to 50% of their partner's qualified income. You can be qualified for benefits via your spouse if you are at least 62 years of age and are caring for a child (a child being anyone below 19). The spousal benefit could equal up to 50% of the partner's benefit, depending on when the working partner retires.

Even divorcees can apply. In fact, spousal payments premised on the other spouse's social security earnings are available to both parties in the case of divorce.

You cannot, however, get your ex-partner's benefits if you have since married someone else.

4. Receive a Dependent Benefit

If you have dependents younger than 19, they are entitled to up to 50 percent of your income if you are retired. The amount of Social Security payments a parent can get is unaffected by this dependent benefit.

They are just added to the family's social security package, meaning you get a bigger check.

5. Monitor Your Earnings

Stay on top of your earnings and keep a close eye on them if you continue working after receiving Social Security benefits to ensure they don't exceed the permitted amount.

For recipients who aren't yet at full retirement age (FRA), the cap on earned income for 2022 is $19,560; for those who are, it's $51,960. These figures increase to $21,240 for those below FRA and $56,520 for the year they reach it, for 2023.

If you go over these restrictions, your benefit payout is lowered for the entire year. However, no penalties exist for income earned at any level until you reach FRA.

5. Watch for a Tax-Bracket Bump

Your income and Social Security benefits may raise your tax bracket. Of course, if you make enough more money, the bracket bump-up might not be as significant as the extra money you're getting, so you need to consider this too. You must be on the lookout for a tax-bracket raise if you continue to work while collecting assistance.

6. Apply for Survivor Benefits

You may qualify for a greater survivor benefit if your deceased spouse (or ex-spouse) qualified for a more significant Social Security benefit than you. Even in the case that your spouse passed away before they got to apply for their benefits, you can still be eligible for the greater benefit.

A word of caution: If you start receiving Social Security benefits before you hit the full retirement age, your benefit will be lowered, and your surviving spouse will also get a lower amount upon your passing.

7. Check for Mistakes

Every year, you receive a Social Security statement.

Do not take it for granted that it's accurate. Verify the figures and notify the Social Security Administration of any mistakes you find (and best believe, many folks find errors).

Remember that the aggregate of your 35 best earning years determines your benefits. Even just one or even two of those years' computations being wrong will likely have long-term effects on your benefit.

8. Change Your Mind

The option to stop receiving benefits, repay any money you have already received, and resume receiving benefits later may be available. You are eligible for this as long as you have collected benefits for less than one year.

You can suspend your benefits if you receive an inheritance or get a job after retirement, and decide you can wait to file for benefits to receive a larger payout in the future. To accomplish this, submit your Form 521, Request for Withdrawal of Application, from the Social Security Administration.

Your benefit ought to be significantly bigger when you resubmit your application later.

Here is what other folks like you have to say on the same:

1. Ed Caruthers, 43, says:

"There are two ways.

Making additional money while you're working is one method that definitely works. Take a job that entails SS tax payment. To be eligible for the maximum SS benefits, you must earn and pay enough taxes.

Waiting as long as you can before claiming benefits is another strategy that might work. Take note of the phrase "may work." The length of your life will determine if you truly receive additional rewards. If you pass away before you can begin collecting, you obviously loose.

81 was the crossing point when I once calculated the figures, and if you lived past 81, the later you began receiving benefits, the more money you got. But if you pass away before age 81, you get less money, obviously. And that was just an interest-free computation in absolute dollars. One

of the basic tenets of finance is that "money now is quite a bit better than money later."

2. **David Frailey, 56, says:**

"How long the beneficiary of those benefits will live is a factor. Naturally, you can't know that beforehand. However, you might have access to enough details to generate a reliable estimate.

For instance, there is a good possibility that you will live a long life if your parents did. However, your life expectancy could be significantly shorter than normal if you lead a dangerous lifestyle, drink or smoke heavily, or have significant medical disorders.

In general, you should put off taking social security benefits the longer you anticipate living. Because you'll have more years to receive the greater benefits, your benefits will increase. On the other hand, you would be better off taking social security earlier if you anticipate living a significantly shorter life than normal.

If you truly don't know how long you are going to live, you also should consider that social security has a very significant benefit: it provides guaranteed income for the duration of your life and is annually adjusted for inflation.

It serves as protection from financial ruin. I decided to wait till age 70 to begin receiving benefits because I reasoned that if I live into my 90s or beyond, I will very much appreciate having larger payouts from social security."

Retirement Planning

3. **Frederick Reinders, 48, says:**

"If you're wondering how to get the most benefit possible given your recent SSA note that:

You will receive the highest pension payout possible based on your employment history if you retire at age 70. Your pension check will be reduced if you retire before the Full Retirement Age (FRA), with the penalty starting at age 62. Up until the age of 70, there will be a little (2/3 percent) monthly boost for retiring after FRA, after which there'll be no more increments for pension delay."

"Your expected lifespan will determine when you decide to retire within this eight-year period to optimize lifetime earnings.

Age 70 retirement will pay the most if you anticipate living into your late 80s or beyond, whereas early retirement will pay the most if you expect to pass away at a younger age owing to, say, chronic medical issues."

Verdict

The points at which each option "crosses over" and gets less profitable than other options are shown in these tables:

Early or late retirement (Explanation on SSA website):

Year of birth	Delayed retirement credit Credit per year
1917-24	3.0%
1925-26	3.5%
1927-28	4.0%
1929-30	4.5%
1931-32	5.0%
1933-34	5.5%
1935-36	6.0%
1937-38	6.5%
1939-40	7.0%
1941-42	7.5%
1943 and later	8.0%

Early or delayed retirement (Spreadsheet: *Effect of Early or Delayed Retirement on Retirement Benefits*):

Benefit, as a percentage of Primary Insurance Amount (PIA), payable at ages 62-67 and age 70

Year of birth	Normal Retirement Age (NRA)	Credit for each year of delayed retirement after NRA (percent)	Benefit, as a percentage of PIA, beginning at age--						
			62	63	64	65	66	67	70
1924	65	3	80	86 2/3	93 1/3	100	103	106	115
1925-26	65	3 1/2	80	86 2/3	93 1/3	100	103 1/2	107	117 1/2
1927-28	65	4	80	86 2/3	93 1/3	100	104	108	120
1929-30	65	4 1/2	80	86 2/3	93 1/3	100	104 1/2	109	122 1/2
1931-32	65	5	80	86 2/3	93 1/3	100	105	110	125
1933-34	65	5 1/2	80	86 2/3	93 1/3	100	105 1/2	111	127 1/2
1935-36	65	6	80	86 2/3	93 1/3	100	106	112	130
1937	65	6 1/2	80	86 2/3	93 1/3	100	106 1/2	113	132 1/2
1938	65, 2 mo.	6 1/2	79 1/6	85 5/9	92 2/9	98 8/9	105 5/12	111 11/12	131 5/12
1939	65, 4 mo.	7	78 1/3	84 4/9	91 1/9	97 7/9	104 2/3	111 2/3	132 2/3
1940	65, 6 mo.	7	77 1/2	83 1/3	90	96 2/3	103 1/2	110 1/2	131 1/2
1941	65, 8 mo.	7 1/2	76 2/3	82 2/9	88 8/9	95 5/9	102 1/2	110	132 1/2
1942	65, 10 mo.	7 1/2	75 5/6	81 1/9	87 7/9	94 4/9	101 1/4	108 3/4	131 1/4
1943-54	66	8	75	80	86 2/3	93 1/3	100	108	132
1955	66, 2 mo.	8	74 1/6	79 1/6	85 5/9	92 2/9	98 8/9	106 2/3	130 2/3
1956	66, 4 mo.	8	73 1/3	78 1/3	84 4/9	91 1/9	97 7/9	105 1/3	129 1/3
1957	66, 6 mo.	8	72 1/2	77 1/2	83 1/3	90	96 2/3	104	128
1958	66, 8 mo.	8	71 2/3	76 2/3	82 2/9	88 8/9	95 5/9	102 2/3	126 2/3

These tables of monthly payments at retirement options can be created using the percentages outlined in the latter table and a spreadsheet program like LibreOffice Calc to help you decide what retirement age is ideal for you.

Remember that benefits received before FRA are regarded differently than those received following FRA and may be taxable as a result. (For further information on the tax liability, see IRS Form 1040 instructions.)

There is no universal solution, as there is with the majority of government programs. Based on your personal circumstances, you'll need to conduct an evaluation of the various options.

Include spousal benefits if you're married, even collecting them early and transitioning to employee benefits later for you and your spouse.

Check the guidelines for spousal benefits in the circumstance that you have been widowed or divorced. You might be able to begin receiving spousal benefits on their behalf and eventually transition to employee benefits on your behalf.

The Bottom Line

Benefits from Social Security are an essential component of retirement preparation. Perhaps you have more rights and benefits than you realize. You can increase your monthly payment when you begin collecting retirement benefits by simultaneously putting a few of the aforementioned measures into practice.

The previous chapter covered the various plans, and in several of them, you're tasked with personally deciding what your investments are. The next chapter looks at how you can invest your retirement funds to maximize your retirement money.

Chapter 8: How to Invest for Retirement

We'll fly straight off the handle with this one: given how much of a role compounding has with retirement planning and the sheer number of years to work with, you want to make sound investments, starting now, all the way to your retirement. These may not always be the most promising ones and may not always have the highest upside.

There may be other investment options that have way more potential to multiply your money. But making sound investments over a long period will almost always make you more money than lose you.

A sound investment choice is one that yields more returns than risks. It is that investment with a lower standard deviation, which is the amount by which it has historically moved around its average when given the option between two assets with historical twenty-year annualized average returns of 7 percent each. (7% is the figure you want to cap your returns at, as anything lower than this becomes too inefficient by default to take seriously).

Sometimes though, you need to take more risk and eschew the safer investment. While taking on too much risk can be damaging, it can also result in great potential benefits. The idea is to have your portfolio dominated by sound investments that fit the description we gave above.

This is particularly true for retired folks, who depend on regular, recurring withdrawals from their investment portfolios to supplement their income, and who do not have as much time to tinker around and make risky plays as younger folks. The worst-case scenario to prevent in this situation is premature financial exhaustion.

Therefore, it is crucial to maintain low portfolio volatility and lessen the severity of collapses. The need to guarantee that long-term returns surpass inflation must be weighed against this.

Social Security retirement payments will replace only around 40 percent of your pre-retirement revenue. You will need to add a pension, savings, or investments to your benefits. Many retirees look for part-time work for a variety of reasons, such as the psychological and financial advantages of continuing to be involved and active in their communities. But you should still have a solid plan in place for bringing in extra money in retirement.

Here are 7 retirement investing options that, when combined as a part of a well-diversified investment portfolio, provide a favorable risk-return profile:

1. Annuities

An annuity, which is a contract between you and your insurance provider, outlines the terms under which you will pay a lump sum and get recurring payments in return. You can use annuities to create a guaranteed stream of income for the remainder of your life or for a specific amount of time.

You pay a certain sum to an insurance provider with the assumption that you will get the funds later via recurring payments. The money could potentially grow tax-deferred while it is with your insurance company.

Once you begin receiving payments, you may decide on a steady income source or adjust your expenses to keep up with inflation. You can also choose whether this income will be paid throughout your life alone or over the lifetimes of you and someone else (e.g., your spouse).

The total investment amount will be returned to you or your beneficiaries and heirs under the liquidity provisions of many annuities.

Regardless of market swings, annuities can offer:

- A consistent, predictable income source in retirement.
- Tax-advantaged income and tax-deferred growth.
- Flexibility in your retirement financial planning and distribution strategies.
- The possibility of payments to beneficiaries after your death.

Annuities' drawbacks include the fact that:

- Guarantees are dependent on the underlying insurance company's capacity to pay claims.
- There may not be much liquidity.
- Annuity withdrawals made before 59½ will incur a 10% tax penalty.

- The risks could be higher if a reputable insurance provider does not underwrite your annuity.

2. Total return investment approach

With this one, the revenue from your portfolio is provided through a total return strategy in the form of dividends, interest, and capital gains. This kind of portfolio makes investments in a well-balanced, varied selection of bond and equity funds.

Rather than concentrating on particular yearly return rates or only using portfolio income, "total" return in this sense refers to spending a percentage of the annual average rate of returns, which includes income and appreciation, over a longer time frame (10–20 years). The goal is to have a total return equal to or greater than your withdrawal rate.

According to Rob Haworth, executive asset allocation director at U.S. Bank, "this is a way to develop a retirement portfolio to satisfy the needs of folks planning for a retirement that may span twenty to thirty years or longer. In comparison to other investment strategies typically used in retirement, it could present a chance to earn a higher total return."

With regard to the rate of withdrawal, a total return plan adopts a "systematic withdrawal" strategy whereby a specific portion of your investment funds is distributed each year. Typically, the distribution amount falls between 3 percent and 5 percent of the portfolio's entire value.

A total return approach may provide:

- A means to satisfy your current cash flow requirements while continuing to accumulate money for future expenditures, which are sure to increase over time, owing to inflation.

- A wider range of assets can be used, which is impossible with more traditional methods of generating retirement income.

- A steady stream of investment portfolio withdrawals could be more advantageous tax-wise because they can be predominantly driven by capital growth.

Retirement Planning

Challenges of a total return approach:

- Money will not necessarily last you through retirement, especially if you retire early.

- Your exact return amount may change from one year to the next (there is no capped withdrawal rate).

- In situations where investments see considerable reductions in value during the initial retirement years, assets may run out before the end of retirement.

3. Publicly-traded real estate investment trusts (REITs)

Real estate is quite the enticing investment prospect for retirees looking to make money. For the majority, investing in REITs is a more practical choice, although you can own and oversee rental properties personally.

This investment vehicle resembles a co-mingled fund (a fund that includes all kinds of company stocks) in specific ways. Still, instead of owning stocks, it makes investments in different types of real estate that generate income.

Publicly traded REITs can be bought and sold just like stocks because they are listed on significant stock exchanges. Daily price changes also occur, just as is the case with stocks. According to Rob Haworth, investors should consider these price fluctuations because they affect the price in ways more than only the fundamental value of the properties held by the REIT.

External variables that influence the broader environment for investment may impact the price at which you purchase a REIT or the price at which you sell a REIT.

REITs frequently concentrate on particular property types (e.g., residential properties, office space, warehouse/industrial space, and so on) and make money from income collected from tenants of the assets they control. Most REITs fall within the equity REIT category and concentrate on producing consistent income from rental assets. If properties are sold, there may be some opportunity for capital growth.

Loans to other operators and owners of real estate are how mortgage REITs make money. Both approaches are combined in hybrid REITs.

Publicly-traded REITs can provide:

- A consistent stream of income which can help with a long-term cash flow plan for retirement.

- Diversification of your investment portfolio primarily comprised of bonds and stocks.

- A resource that is easily bought or sold on the market.

- The chance to pick from a variety of REITs, each with a particular financial strategy.

Challenges of publicly-traded REITs:

- Daily price variations, which often do not reflect the actual value of the properties purchased but rather other market conditions, can affect the investment's intrinsic worth.

- Limited opportunity for capital growth; as REITs must distribute 90% of their income to investors, there is little money left over for reinvestment.

- Ordinary tax rates on earnings are often higher for income obtained by investors.

- REIT management fees can be higher than those for other managed types of investment, like mutual funds.

4. **Non-Traded Real Estate Investment Trusts (Non-Traded REITs)**

You can invest in a professionally-managed investment portfolio of commercial property through a non-traded REIT. Investors typically hold this non-liquid asset for the trust's duration until the management group sells it. It differs from publicly-traded REITs in this way because they cannot be bought or sold on open marketplaces.

Vacation homes, shopping malls, apartment complexes, hotels, data centers, warehouses, medical facilities, office buildings, and forests could all be included in a non-traded REIT portfolio. Infrastructure such as cellular towers, oil and gas pipelines, and broadband cables are possible further investments.

Non-traded REITs tend to concentrate on just one kind of property (be it shopping malls, data centers, etc.).

There are professionals who actively manage these portfolios and receive payment for their services (we'll discuss these professionals in a separate chapter.) After paying expenditures and collecting rent from the properties, the managers give investors any remaining money in the form of dividends.

According to Rob Haworth, non-traded REITs aren't impacted by daily price fluctuation as opposed to publicly traded REITs. He, however, issues a warning that non-traded REITs may encounter specific difficulties during times of economic downturn. "Investors need to view this as a long-term investment because challenging circumstances which are detrimental to the real estate marketplace in general can occasionally develop, throwing things off balance if you approached it as a shorter-term investment."

Non-Traded REITs can provide:

- Possibility of making money from real estate without necessarily having to take care of property management.

- The capacity to acquire a stake in several unconventional property kinds, such as forests, data centers, etc.

- A consistent source of revenue (at least in most kinds of non-traded REITs).

- Diversification for your investment portfolio primarily comprised of bonds and stocks.

Challenges of Non-Traded REITs:

- Have significant administration and transaction costs.

- Non-traded REITs have little liquidity; you are either obligated to stay invested for the whole period of the REIT or pay penalties for leaving early.

- There can only be an investment in one market segment.

- Subject to shifts in the state of the global, regional, and local economies, including changes in interest rates and inflation.

- They are investments that are difficult to understand and that have strict net worth and income requirements.

5. Income-producing equities

While the main reason people invest in stocks is to increase the value of their portfolio, some stocks also generate earnings in the form of dividends. Dividend payments are a common way for publicly traded firms to distribute their profits to their shareholders. Specific equities typically pay more enormous dividends than others among the stocks that pay dividends, whereas not all stocks do.

"When we faced an exceptionally low rate of interest environment in the bond market, stock dividends became considerably more attractive," says Rob Haworth. It can be a good strategy to diversify your sources of income and produce returns that are competitive.

Quarterly dividend payments are the norm for stock dividends. Companies occasionally might pay a "special dividend" due to exceptional circumstances, but this is rare and isn't something you should anticipate. However, stock dividends can change for each passing period when payouts are issued, unlike most bonds. With dividend payouts, you must be ready for a certain amount of uncertainty.

If your main goal is to invest in a particular stock for revenue, it's critical to examine the stock's dividend payment history. For this reason, the most appealing stocks to consider are probably those with a track record of stable or continuously rising dividend payouts (remember what we said about making sound investments?)

Income-producing equities can provide:

- A stable source of income provided by businesses that have high earnings and consistently pay out dividends.

- The chance to profit from the potential capital growth of equities that also produce income.

- A "built-in return" on the investment portfolio, irrespective of the success of the stock's price.

- A variety of income sources for your retirement portfolio.

Challenges with income-producing stocks:

- The principal value is more susceptible to change than other conventional income sources like bonds.
- Not all businesses consistently and dependably pay out dividends.
- With rising interest rates, stock dividends might lose some of their appeal.
- Higher ordinary rates of income tax apply to dividend income.

Your timeline and risk tolerance level should be considered when choosing your retirement investment choices. You can better comprehend these possibilities with the aid of a financial expert, who can also help you decide whether one or more of them is suitable for your income strategy for retirement.

We will look at working with a financial advisor for your retirement investments in the next chapter. But basically, you will be better prepared to enter (or remain in) your years of retirement with confidence and minimal worry if you have a better understanding of your investment options and overall financial situation.

Here are 4 more low-risk, high-reward investments you can make to ensure your retirement goes swimmingly:

Low-Volatility Stocks

According to the capital asset pricing model, a stock's predicted future return is based on how exposed it is to systematic risk, often known as market risk. We may put it this way: greater risk equals greater reward. This is why investing in stocks, as opposed to bonds, typically yields a higher long-term return.

A major exception exists, nevertheless, in the instance of low-volatility equities. These equities are less sensitive to changes in the larger market than, for example, the S&P 500 in terms of standard deviation and beta.

Low-volatility stocks have historically outperformed the market, particularly large-cap ones with strong, solid fundamentals. By concentrating on blue-chip, dividend-paying, low-volatility stocks, retirees could reduce the risk of their portfolio allocation without significantly lowering their expected returns.

Preferred Stock

Preferred stock is a product with both fixed-income and equity features. Preferred equities have preferential access to a corporation's assets over ordinary shares in the case of bankruptcy or liquidation.

They don't have any voting rights, though. However, preferred stock frequently offers a greater and more reliable fixed dividend in exchange. The corporation may be required to make dividend payouts in arrears if they are not made on time under certain circumstances.

Preferred stock has a risk-return profile similar to bonds due to the consistency of cash flows. In general, preferred stock carries a greater interest rate risk than regular stock and more negligible market risk than bonds.

Preferred stock can be purchased individually by investors or in a portfolio using exchange-traded funds (ETFs), such as the iShares Preferred & Income Securities ETF (PFF).

Bond Ladders

Retirement investors frequently own sizable amounts of investment-grade corporate bonds and Treasury securities.

Bonds are highly vulnerable to interest rate risk, as we touched on in the previous investment kind, despite generally carrying less risk compared to stocks. Bond yields climb in response to rising rates, which lowers bond prices. This is particularly true for bonds with longer maturities.

Bond laddering is a strategy for protecting your portfolio against interest rate risk. This entails purchasing numerous bonds with varied/staggered maturities. Investors can redeem each bond at maturity for its face value, eliminating the need to do so at a loss if interest rates are rising. Bond ladders guarantee more consistent cash flows, which is essential for retirees taking planned income withdrawals.

Certificates of Deposit (CDs)

A CD is a savings vehicle that financial institutions offer which guarantees both the principal and a fixed yearly interest rate for the lifespan of your investment.

You can choose a lock-up rate or the length of time during which you are unable to redeem your investment when you put money into a CD. The CD will give you a yearly rate of interest during this period. You get your upfront outlay back at maturity.

As of 2022, CDs are offering competitive yields above standard savings and money market accounts, with some exceeding 2.7%, due to growing interest rates. With your money protected by the Federal Deposit Insurance Corp., CDs are as dependable and risk-free as it gets. Retirees can create a pyramid of CDs with varying maturities, as in the case of bond laddering, to ensure consistent cash flows.

We've touched on working with a financial advisor several times in this chapter. The next chapter discusses streamlining your investments, working with these professionals, how to vet them, so you settle on the best possible pick and more.

Chapter 9: Streamline Your Retirement Income Sources

Efficiency is key. The higher your efficacy levels are when putting your portfolio together, the more streamlined and risk-free it will be, and the easier it will be for your retirement plan to hold up to unexpected financial storms.

Those of us who are just starting our retirement investment journey may find the process of constructing an investment portfolio daunting. Budgeting for the numerous bills that come with being a functional, responsible adult, including rent, equivalent monthly installments (EMIs) for our cars, and other commitments, might make it challenging to set aside enough money each month. But the sooner you start investing, the more time your portfolio has to develop and grow, and allow you an easy, worry-free retirement.

Smart investments ensure that you can prepare for your short- and long-term objectives while taking into consideration your current expenses. The balance between growth potential and dangers is the most crucial component of portfolio construction. The secret is developing a diversified portfolio while being aware of your risk tolerance.

Here are several tips to put together a robust, streamlined investment portfolio.

Pointers to Build a Robust Investment PortfolioAsset Allocation

You want to have a diversified investment portfolio to streamline your retirement plan and safeguard it against unexpected setbacks. Investing in various assets, such as bonds, stocks, government securities, commodities, real estate, and cash, is the most fundamental rule of portfolio construction.

A prudent asset mix of securities and equities will be essential for protecting your portfolio against a decline in a certain asset or market. Your investment goals, investment horizon, and risk tolerance are the three primary factors you must take into account while allocating assets.

1. **Financial goals**

It will help to evaluate your short-, mid-, and long-term investment objectives before you start putting together your portfolio. Vacations and home renovations are goals that can be completed in less than 3 years. Those will be your short-term objectives.

Mid-term objectives can be set for 3 to 10 years, and may include things like paying for your children's college education. Long-term objectives like saving for retirement or purchasing a home will typically take well over 10 years to complete. Therefore, your investment strategy and asset allocation should be in line with these objectives.

2. Investment horizon

This is the length of time that you plan to hold onto an investment. Your financial objectives should guide your choice of the different assets in your portfolio's investment horizon.

Assets that will bloom in time for your short-, mid-, and long-term objectives should be in your portfolio – try and avoid a situation where you have too many short-term objective assets or too many long-term ones. Balance is a key factor to have.

3. Risk tolerance

Risk tolerance is the amount of risk you can tolerate, influenced by your income, spending, and risk-taking propensity. It may vary from one individual to the next and alter over time.

Your risk tolerance, for example, can rise as your income rises and falls if your dependents and expenditures grow. Age might also affect risk tolerance, as typically, folks who are getting near retirement will, quite understandably, be less inclined to accept high risk.

Understand just how much risk you're willing to stomach and then set about putting your portfolio together.

4. Risk diversification

Risk diversification is one of the foundational principles of a wise investment. Based on the idea that varied assets have varying degrees of risk, it entails investments across a range of assets to lessen the risk impact related to any one asset class. Investments with little risk often have poor returns, whereas those with significant risk frequently have larger returns.

We can balance our security and risk by investing in various asset classes. Each asset class needs to be subject to diversification. According to risk diversification, low-risk, low-return assets like market securities and bonds ought to be used to offset the investment risks in high-growth companies, in order to achieve the best returns. By limiting the financial impact, diversifying your investments across several markets and businesses protects your investment portfolio from an unexpected nosedive in these areas.

Basically, we're saying that it is vital that you have a balanced portfolio as far as taking risks goes. If you're the free-wheeling, risk-taking type, it may be very tempting to stock up on high-risk, high-reward securities.

The problem with this is that the higher proclivity to setbacks can bring you to your knees financially very quickly. It is far better – far wiser, too – to have a healthy mix of low-risk and high-risk investments.

Speaking of risk, let's look at minimizing portfolio risks:

Minimizing Portfolio Risks

A portfolio will inevitably have risks attached to it – all portfolios, even the most astutely put together, have a risk load. Wise investment emphasizes risk management to reduce your exposure to risks via risk diversification (covered above). It is regarded as the best tactic for managing all risk factors.

You can reduce your exposure to sovereign risks by ensuring that your investment portfolio doesn't rely primarily on government assets for stability. Sovereign risks include things like wars, political storms, and the like, which could have devastating effects on the economy and financial market.

While mutual funds and bonds – low-risk investments – are great for balancing out the likelihood of principal loss, diversifying into typically high-risk equities like stocks can go a long way in minimizing inflation risk.

Investors must simultaneously watch for changes in the market. Stop-loss orders are one strategy used to minimize losses in cases where they cannot be avoided.

The routine evaluation and rebalancing of an investment portfolio is another crucial component of risk management. Depending on our age, income, and personal circumstances, our risk tolerance may (and will) change over time. For instance, you won't be as eager to take as many risks when you have kids or are getting close to retirement.

It's critical to analyze your portfolio to discover how much of it is made up of low-risk, low-return securities like bonds, mutual funds, and fixed-income securities and high-risk, high-return investments like stocks.

With this covered, let's glean into working with a financial advisor:

Working with a Financial Advisor to Further Streamline Your Portfolio

Let's start right off the top with this one:

Who Are Financial Advisors?

Let's face it, not all of us have the interest or the time to become financial experts. Still, being able to handle finances on an individual and household level is becoming more and more crucial every day.

But don't worry. You can consider hiring a financial advisor if you want to have a straightforward, low-maintenance (at least on your end) strategy that you can carry out without having to continually track and fret over modifications in the law, the economy, or financial products.

Understanding Financial Advisors & What they Do

So, who are financial advisors, and what's their deal? Financial advisors are financial experts who give their clients advice on choices involving personal money and asset management.

Financial advisors will aid you with anything from creating a comprehensive savings plan for retirement with a schedule tied to it to just responding to an inquiry regarding whole life insurance. The services they give you will, of course, depend on their specific area of expertise.

Here is a list of some of the services a financial advisor can provide:

- Meet with you to discuss your financial situation as of right now and your long-term objectives.

- Put together a concise strategy that takes into account your main financial concerns, such as retirement, college preparation, insurance, avoiding estate taxes, etc.

- Give guidance as unforeseen financial challenges in your life emerge.

- Create investment accounts and make investments on your behalf.

- Find the right investment vehicles for you (we've already looked at these)

Pros and Cons of Hiring a Financial Advisor

Let's start with the perks of hiring a financial advisor or planner:

Pros of Hiring a Financial Advisor

Financial planners can greatly help when you are uncertain, upset, or simply ill-informed about numerous money management issues. Professional counsel can be quite helpful, especially given that most folks cannot envision their retirement, let alone make plans for it, in the far future.

A qualified advisor will ask you lots of questions—some of which may be uncomfortable – to fully understand where you want to go in your life, financially speaking.

The financial advisor will then put together a strategy and guide you on investments, retirement planning, estate planning, tax liabilities, and your children's college expenses once all the specifics are known.

The depth of the advisor's understanding may greatly simplify a lot of financial issues that you regard to be challenging or confusing. You can think of a financial advisor as a coach, drawing up complex plays behind the scenes and making them straightforward for your execution.

Cons of Hiring a Financial Advisor

A terrible financial counselor can be just as effective as a good one, in a negative way, of course. You could lose a lot of money if your advisor is subpar or, even worse, dishonest. When working with a financial advisor, keep an eye out for the following warning signs:

1) Your investments being churned: Some advisors encourage clients to purchase and sell assets more frequently than necessary to increase their commissions.

2) Expensive investments: They might recommend mutual funds featuring high fee ratios when an exchange-traded fund (ETF) or a comparable index fund with a lower expense ratio would be a better option.

3) Poor planning: A well-intentioned counselor who creates a financial plan that is hazy or full of gaps and holes is doing you absolutely no good. Plans must, of course, be adaptable in light of shifting economic conditions, fluctuating interest rates, and potential personal setbacks (job loss, chronic illness, etc.). But you must begin with a thorough plan and a distinct line of action.

Choosing a Financial Advisor: Key Questions to Ask

Here are several questions you must ask prospective financial advisors so you can make the ideal pick:

1) Do they have expertise working with clients similar to you? This may apply to retirees, same-sex couples, divorcées, surviving spouses, women, Black or Indigenous Persons of Color (BIPOC), LGBTQ+ persons, or any other niche that may be relevant.

2) What are their rates and payment methods? Do they expect to profit financially from your investments as a client, as opposed to just charging a management fee?

3) Do they only provide planning, or do they also provide active management?

4) How frequently do they meet with clients to assess the portfolio, plan, or circumstance?

5) How often and how exactly will they get in touch with you? Are there any restrictions on how often you can call them?

The advisory industry is evolving as well. Since most investors now have electronic access to their financial accounts, they can conduct some or even all of their investment portfolio review sessions remotely in addition to the more conventional in-person meetings. Enquire about this too, and get to know if you can schedule Zoom calls every so often.

Paying Your Financial Advisor

We need to talk about this one too. You will have to pay for a professional financial advisor if you want to receive high-quality guidance. Some advisors have defined pricing for particular services or charge by the hour. This is known as fee-based or fee-only planning. Some earn a commission each time they conduct business with you or persuade you to buy anything, and some advisors are paid in both ways.

As opposed to commission-based suggestions, fee-based consultants frequently assert that their counsel is greater since it is free from conflicts of interest (earning money from commissions, etc.).

Commission-based advisors respond by claiming that their services are considerably less expensive compared to paying fees which can sometimes be as exorbitant as $100 an hour or more.

They also argue that you are paying for "demonstrated" activities and services, not simply vague advice or unclear work hours (seeing as you cannot determine what hours a day your fee-only advisor is working).

You will need to decide the best option for you. Take your time and use the questionnaire we provided.

Next up, we look at proofing your retirement financially.

Chapter 10: How To Proof Your Retirement Financially

Zoe Heelwani, a 2nd generation US citizen of Jewish descent, tells a moving story of her own experience:

"I tried asking my mom if they had any arrangements to provide for her if dad passed away. Dad was quite a few years older than she was, with both inching ever closer toward the close of their life, and his health was considerably poorer than hers.

She avoided even contemplating it for clear emotional reasons. I tried not to press her on the subject. Two years later, dad died, and we had to act quickly to ensure mom had enough money to keep enjoying her twilight years.

When Dad passed away, his pension and his benefits from social security were cut by more than 40 percent, while costs decreased by 20 percent. You can imagine just how amplified the stress in our lives was. It was an extremely difficult time for us."

This chapter will show you how to financially proof your retirement so that shocks like the above-illustrated one do not deal devastating financial blows when you're retired and cannot work anymore. We will cover the most important things to have straightened out and wrap up with how to bounce back in the event of a financial setback.

We'll start with emergency funds and having one in place.

1. **Emergency funds**

The lifestyle you are currently leading may no longer be feasible tomorrow or perhaps in a few years, which could be devastating for you. You set aside money in an emergency fund to prepare for unforeseen life situations. If you have ever found yourself in a case where you required instant financial aid, then you understand how crucial it is to create an emergency fund.

Your general financial well-being depends greatly on emergency cash; it's typically advised to have enough money to cover your bills for 3 to 6 months. However, for most of us, that sum may be daunting, which deters even the most well-intentioned saver from buckling up and saving in earnest.

When you have an emergency fund in place, you get to stop worrying about how and where you'll get cash in case of a financial disaster. Can you see just how liberating that is?

Once you're ready for unforeseen life problems, you are confident that your finances and way of life are secure and that you'll be able to get back on track in case of setbacks.

Let's now look at life insurance.

2. Buying life insurance

You may be familiar with life insurance. You might have been advised to purchase it by your mom or spouse, looked around for coverage, or have life insurance via your job. However, are you fully cognizant of what life insurance really is and the benefits it may provide for you and your loved ones?

The people who rely on you should immediately come to mind if you ask yourself, "Why do I need to acquire life insurance?" Life insurance is a way to financially support and safeguard them, making it a crucial (and frequently surprisingly affordable) component of any financial plan, retirement or otherwise.

Take Zoe Heelwani's example early in the chapter. If her dad had set about buying life insurance when he was younger and able to earn his keep, his family would have had far fewer financial worries when his health started to fail and he eventually passed.

A little financial planning is necessary at every stage of your life to achieve your goals. Consider your greatest financial aspirations, such as purchasing a home, sending your children to college, or setting up money for retirement. Life insurance can defend against the unforeseen as you and your family save up for these milestones.

Life insurance will ensure your family gets a tax-free lump sum payout that they can spend for anything and everything they need in the event of your untimely death. That money can be used to pay for everyday expenses, lessen financial obligations, and accomplish the objectives you've been working so hard to reach together.

Don't let ignorance prevent you from safeguarding your family's financial future. Here are the perks of life insurance:

Guaranteed protection

The life insurance benefit of a whole-life policy serves as a safety net for your finances if you have a spouse and children, a business, or others who depend on you.

Your beneficiaries will be given a lump sum that is promised to be paid entirely when you pass away (provided all the premiums have been paid and you have no outstanding loans). It is crucial protection that you can count on to be there for your loved ones in case anything happens to you.

Income replacement

What would happen to your loved ones if something happened to you suddenly? By purchasing whole life insurance, you can ensure that your loved ones have the resources necessary for:

- Mortgage payments
- Paying for daycare, medical care, and other services
- Paying for tuition and other college costs
- Getting rid of personal debt
- Keeping a family company going

Tax-free benefit

Every dollar you leave your dependents will be theirs to keep and enjoy. This is because a life insurance policy's benefit is wired federal income tax-free.

Guaranteed cash value growth

Your Whole Life policy's cash value grows tax-deferred while you pay your premiums, and it can help you achieve a range of financial objectives:

- Finance the education of a child or grandchild to supplement retirement income
- Pay off mortgages
- Safeguard existing assets

- Create a fund for emergencies.

The next item to financially safeguard your retirement is health insurance.

3. Health insurance

Health insurance aids in lowering medical expenses, making medical treatment more accessible and, thus, more inexpensive. Health insurance makes care access easier, which lowers mortality rates and progresses healthcare outcomes.

Therefore, health insurance can fundamentally be the determining factor between severe illness and sound health and even between death and life.

How Health Insurance Works

When you've got medical insurance, your health insurance plan is the first place your medical bills are paid. Then, following the specifics of the plan, they pay all or part of that bill.

Health insurance resembles auto insurance in certain ways. Automobile insurance covers a portion or the entirety of the cost if your vehicle is in a serious accident and requires extensive repairs or perhaps needs to be outright replaced with a brand-new vehicle.

The cost of repairing or replacing your vehicle could easily exceed the amount sitting in your bank account, so that's a good thing.

However, unlike auto insurance, health insurance pays for much more than the costs of an unfortunate accident. Annual physicals, immunizations, preventative care, and other types of "regular maintenance" for your mind and body are typically covered by health insurance. It would be similar to auto insurance paying for tire rotations, and oil changes, which we all know doesn't happen.

Health Insurance as a Safety Net

Health insurance is crucial as a safety net. Health insurance is available to help cover expenditures you probably will not be able to pay on your own if you become ill or injured unexpectedly.

The cost of medical care can be exceptionally high. It could be a huge financial strain. Costs for procedures, including surgery, urgent care, prescription medications, lab work, scans, and exams, can quickly pile up, as you may well know from loved ones or colleagues you know. They

Retirement Planning

may even be excessive enough to force people into bankruptcy or forego necessary care they cannot pay for out of pocket.

But with medical insurance, you don't have to deal with such expenses on your own because you have a plan to help you pay for them and sort through the confusing world of medical billing. To put it simply and pointedly – you NEED life insurance. It mustn't be viewed as an option; it is as much of a necessity as every other item covered here.

Since we've covered all these vital retirement-proofing items, it's time to look at what you must do in the event of an unexpected, devastating financial setback.

How To Pick Yourself Back Up In The Face of a Financial Setback

A financial disaster does not have to negatively impact your physical and mental health, whether you have lost your job or are saddled with hefty medical expenses following an accident.

You may need some time to recover financially, but you must maintain your composure and push to navigate through this trying moment. Here are a few suggestions to aid in your mental recuperation following a financial setback.

1. **Do not overreact.** You will be exposing yourself to even greater financial issues if you tend to rack up expenses when you are under stress or perhaps take more financial risks to recuperate more quickly.

When analyzing your predicament and seeking answers, try to keep your emotions out of the picture.

2. **Find support.** Don't be scared to ask for help if your financial issue is causing you worry or difficulty focusing on other crucial areas of life. You could speak with dependable family members or friends or look for reasonably priced expert assistance.

Pick up the phone and call a counselor, a financial planner, or someone else in your community who can aid you climb out of your rut and getting back on your feet. Many counselors will allow you to pay whatever you can manage until your recovery by offering a sliding range of prices.

3. **Make a concise list of losses**. Although facing the issue head-on might not be simple or easy to do, doing so can help you gain a better understanding of its scope and the potential effects it could have on your objectives.

Analyze the circumstances so you may begin developing a plan to recover those monies and have a good notion of how much you've lost overall. It can also weigh very heavily to keep your financial situation a secret. Get all the information in the open. This will offer you the opportunity to experience the full pain of the loss once and for all so that you can acknowledge and accept your situation as it is now and begin to move on.

4. **Sit down and assess your budget.** It can be significantly more challenging to bounce back from a financial loss if you forget your present budget and payment due dates.

To save money, make a list of your present spending and reassess your priorities. This may make it easier for you to add to your savings. You may also find some comfort from any worry or anxiety you could be feeling regarding your financial condition by reviewing your budget.

5. **Come up with a new vision**. Sometimes taking action and changing your course just requires more than merely thinking of optimistic ideas. If you depended on the funds you lost to accomplish goals like buying a house, paying off your debt by a set deadline, or taking a trip at a specific period, think about coming up with a new vision and set of altered goals with your present financial resources.

Conclusion

This guide is the most comprehensive retirement planning guide on the internet. If you follow all the directives laid out and look to internalize all the nuggets of wisdom outlined, you will have no issues setting up your retirement plan.

You will be able to save up efficiently and be completely confident and relaxed when retirement eventually looms. Better yet, the knowledge contained in this guide will not only help you plan for retirement, but it will help you become a more financially responsible person altogether.

Have a look at how two people, both of whom are in different age categories, are doing to save up for retirement and see what you can learn from them:

Kate Dore, 32

Kate Dore from Nashville has developed a passion for retirement planning. The social media advertising expert frequently updates Cashville Skyline, her personal finance blog, with her net worth. Dore had accumulated upwards of $53,000 in a Roth IRA, as of mid-May of 2022, in addition to over $21,000 in a taxable interest-bearing account.

That's astounding, especially given that the 32-year-old, as she claims, has never made a lot of money per year.

Dore asserts, "*I've always been an ordinary earner. I once held a marketing position in the music industry. I currently work in social media marketing. Rarely have I had access to a 401(k). I want to demonstrate to others that saving for retirement is still possible even if you don't make six figures annually.*"

Dore has only ever had a 401(k) plan in her professional career, which she had while working in advertising for a recording studio. However, she was only employed there for 6 months before being let go. She hasn't had the chance to contribute to a 401(k) savings account for retirement since that time.

Even so, Dore continues to put money aside for his retirement. She has contributed to her Roth IRA every passing year since turning 18. She now makes the maximum annual commitment to this savings account. She also regularly invests in her taxable investing account since, in her opinion, maxing out her Roth IRA is insufficient.

Dore is certain she's on schedule to meet her retirement savings objectives.

"I wasn't making much in my early 20s," Dore remarked. "But even if it was only a small amount, I knew I needed to start saving. I made a $1,000 yearly contribution when I was 18. Even when I was busing tables, I had it in mind. Since then, I've made an effort to help as much as I can."

Oraynab Jwayyed, 45

Oraynab Jwayyed acknowledges that she didn't begin saving for retirement until she was 42.

Retirement was never really in the cards for Jwayyed because she worked as self-employed for most of her adult life.

That has changed. Jwayyed completed her business degree after going back to school. She was able to use a 401(k) account for the first time after landing her first corporate job. She put roughly 20 percent of her earnings into her account at that time.

After that, Jwayyed changed jobs and started performing risk assessments for a mortgage provider. In addition to making contributions to the 401(k)-account provided by her new company, she rolled her prior 401(k) money into an IRA. To assist in managing both funds, Jwayyed has hired a financial advisor. She deposits 10 percent of her income into this new account.

Jwayyed states, "As my pay rises, I intend to channel even more to both funds." "My financial advisor told me my money is working for me. When that time comes, I ought to have sufficient funds to retire."

Final Word

You need to get started immediately, regardless of how old you are. Don't wait for next year or even next month. Get started on your retirement planning right now. Start putting away whatever you can, however little. Be consistent. See if your employer can match your contribution.

Use the knowledge covered here to decide the best retirement account for you. See just how soon you can invest in the investment options recommended in this guide. Use this guide as your foundation and read up even more on the subject. The earlier you get started, the better it will be for you and your loved ones and dependents.

Retirement Planning Worksheets

Here are a few worksheets for you to fill out to further help you in your retirement planning:

Worksheet 1 – Your Retirement Lifestyle

What will your lifestyle be like during retirement? Beside each item listed below, describe what you really want in retirement.

1. Your home: _____

2. Transportation: _____

3. Food: _____

4. Clothing and personal care: _____

5. Health and health care: _____

6. Entertainment: _____

7. Hobbies: _____

8. Recreation: _____

9. Travel: _____

Retirement Planning

Worksheet 2 – Estimated Annual Cost of Living

Fill in the first column with what you are now spending annually to live. Fill in the inflation factor in the second column. (You may do this only for the total, or for each category of costs.) Multiply column 1 by column 2 to get an idea of the income you will need during your first year of retirement.

	Totals You Spend Now	Inflation Factor	Future Budget at Time of Retirement in ____ years
Housing	$		$
Household operation and maintenance	$		$
Automobile and transportation	$		$
Food	$		$
Clothing	$		$
Personal	$		$
Medical and health	$		$
Recreation, education	$		$
Contributions	$		$
Taxes and Insurance	$		$
Savings, investments	$		$
Irregular expenses (ex. gifts, license plates, holiday spending, etc.)	$		$
ANNUAL TOTAL	$		$

Retirement Planning

This table will help you calculate the inflation factor:

Table 1. The Inflation Factor

Years to Retirement	Annual Inflation Rate									
	2%	3%	4%	5%	6%	7%	8%	9%	10%	11%
1	1.02	1.03	1.04	1.05	1.06	1.07	1.08	1.09	1.10	1.11
2	1.04	1.06	1.08	1.10	1.12	1.15	1.17	1.19	1.21	1.23
3	1.06	1.09	1.13	1.16	1.19	1.23	1.26	1.30	1.33	1.37
4	1.08	1.13	1.17	1.22	1.26	1.31	1.36	1.41	1.46	1.52
5	1.10	1.16	1.22	1.28	1.34	1.40	1.47	1.54	1.61	1.69
6	1.13	1.19	1.27	1.34	1.42	1.50	1.59	1.68	1.77	1.87
7	1.15	1.23	1.32	1.41	1.50	1.61	1.71	1.83	1.95	2.08
8	1.17	1.27	1.37	1.48	1.59	1.72	1.85	1.99	2.14	2.30
9	1.20	1.31	1.42	1.55	1.69	1.84	2.00	2.17	2.36	2.56
10	1.22	1.34	1.48	1.63	1.79	1.97	2.16	2.37	2.59	2.84
11	1.24	1.38	1.54	1.71	1.90	2.11	2.33	2.58	2.85	3.15
12	1.27	1.43	1.60	1.80	2.01	2.25	2.52	2.81	3.14	3.50
13	1.29	1.47	1.67	1.89	2.13	2.41	2.72	3.07	3.45	3.88
14	1.32	1.51	1.73	1.98	2.26	2.58	2.94	3.34	3.80	4.31
15	1.35	1.56	1.80	2.08	2.40	2.76	3.17	3.64	4.18	4.78
16	1.37	1.61	1.87	2.18	2.54	2.95	3.43	3.97	4.60	5.31
17	1.40	1.65	1.95	2.29	2.69	3.16	3.70	4.33	5.05	5.90
18	1.43	1.70	2.03	2.41	2.85	3.38	4.00	4.72	5.56	6.54
19	1.46	1.75	2.11	2.53	3.03	3.62	4.32	5.14	6.12	7.26
20	1.49	1.81	2.19	2.65	3.21	3.87	4.66	5.60	6.73	8.06

Retirement Planning

Worksheet 3 – Estimated Changes in Spending After Retirement

Use this worksheet to calculate possible changes in your expenses. For each expense category, figure the difference between what you are spending now and what you expect to spend after retirement. If the retirement expense will be lower, put the difference in the "less" column; if it will be higher, put the difference in the "more" column. Add the figures in both columns and compare the totals. Which total is larger? What does that suggest about your future spending? Will you need to make some changes in what you expect to spend?

Expense	Now Spend About How Much?	Expect to Spend After Retirement	Less After Retirement	More After Retirement
Work related:				
Transportation	$	$	$	$
Clothing	$	$	$	$
Dues	$	$	$	$
Meals	$	$	$	$
Other	$	$	$	$
Social Security taxes (taken out of check)	$	$	$	$
Income taxes	$	$	$	$
Pension plan contributions	$	$	$	$
Contributions to other retirement accounts (IRA, etc.)	$	$	$	$
Savings, investments for retirement	$	$	$	$
Travel	$	$	$	$
Entertainment, leisure activities	$	$	$	$
Health insurance	$	$	$	$
Other health care costs	$	$	$	$
TOTALS			$ Less	$ More

This table outlines expectations of life by age and sex:

Table 2: Expectation of life by age and sex

Age	All Races		
	Total	Male	Female
0	77.4	74.7	80.0
1	77.0	74.3	79.5
5	73.1	70.4	75.6
10	68.1	65.5	70.6
15	63.2	60.5	65.7
20	58.4	55.8	60.8
25	53.6	51.2	56.0
30	48.9	46.5	51.1
35	44.1	41.8	46.3
40	39.5	37.2	41.5
45	34.9	32.8	36.9
50	30.5	28.5	32.3
55	26.2	24.3	27.9
60	22.2	20.4	23.7
65	18.4	16.8	19.7
70	14.8	13.4	15.9
75	11.7	10.5	12.5
80	8.9	7.9	9.5
85	6.6	5.9	7.0
90	4.8	4.3	5.0
95	3.5	3.1	3.5
100	2.5	2.2	2.5

Retirement Planning

Here's the estimated annual living cost 10 years after retirement:

Example: Estimated Annual Cost of Living 10 Years After Retirement

	Your Budget at Retirement	Inflation Factor	Your Budget 10 Years After Retirement
Housing	$17,025	1.63	$27,751
Household operation and maintenance	$3,813	1.63	$6,215
Automobile and transportation	$10,287	1.63	$16,768
Food	$7,726	1.63	$12,593
Clothing	$3,047	1.63	$4,967
Personal	$2,601	1.63	$4,240
Medical and health	$2,847	1.63	$4,641
Recreation, education	$2,837	1.63	$4,624
Contributions	$1,262	1.63	$2,057
Taxes and insurance	$1,902	1.63	$3,100
Savings, investments	$1,333	1.63	$2,173
Irregular expenses (ex. gifts, license plates, holiday spending, etc.)	$513	1.63	$836
ANNUAL TOTAL	$55,194	1.63	$89,966

Worksheet 4 – Estimated Annual Cost of Living 10 Years After Retirement

	Your Budget at Retirement	Inflation Factor	Your Budget 10 Years After Retirement
Housing	$		$
Household operation and maintenance	$		$
Automobile and transportation	$		$
Food	$		$
Clothing	$		$
Personal	$		$
Medical and health	$		$
Recreation, education	$		$
Contributions	$		$
Taxes and insurance	$		$
Savings, investments	$		$
Irregular expenses (ex. gifts, license plates, holiday spending, etc.)	$		$
ANNUAL TOTAL	$		$

Worksheet 5 – Large Future Irregular Expenses

	Year Bought	Average Expected Years of Life	Year to Replace	Present Replacement Price	*Estimated Price in Replacement Year
Vehicles:					
Car	_____	?	_____	$ _____	$ _____
Other vehicles	_____	?	_____	$ _____	$ _____
Appliances:					
Range	_____	12-13	_____	$ _____	$ _____
Refrigerator	_____	15	_____	$ _____	$ _____
Dishwasher	_____	11	_____	$ _____	$ _____
Washer	_____	11	_____	$ _____	$ _____
Dryer	_____	13-14	_____	$ _____	$ _____
Freezer	_____	20	_____	$ _____	$ _____
Furnace	_____	25-30	_____	$ _____	$ _____
Water heater	_____	12	_____	$ _____	$ _____
Other	_____	_____	_____	$ _____	$ _____
House:					
Roof (varies with type)	_____	15-30	_____	$ _____	$ _____
Fencing	_____	20-30	_____	$ _____	$
Other	_____	_____	_____	$	$ _____
	_____	_____	_____	$ _____	$ _____
Furnishings:					
Carpet	_____	8-15	_____	$ _____	$ _____
Drapes, window treatments	_____	10	_____	$ _____	$ _____
Flooring, hard surface	_____	15	_____	$	$
Furniture	_____	will vary	_____	$ _____	$ _____
Other	_____	_____		$ _____	$ _____

Retirement Planning

Worksheet 6 – How Much Are You Worth?

Name_____ Date _____

Assets		Liabilities	
Cash and cash equivalents:		Past due bills for services, rent, etc.	$
Cash on hand	$	Credit cards/charge accounts:	
Checking account(s)	$		$
Savings account(s)	$		$
Certificate of deposit (CD)	$		$
Savings bonds	$		$
Treasury securities	$		$
Money market funds/Money market deposit accounts	$		$
Investment assets:		**Consumer installment debt:**	
Stocks	$	Automobile	$
Bonds	$	Other	$
Mutual funds	$	Real estate debt:	$
Real estate:	$	Home	$
Home	$	Other	$
Other	$	Taxes	$
Cash value of life insurance/annuities	$	Pledges: charities, churches, etc.	$
Partnership and business interest	$	**Other:**	
Retirement assets:			$
IRA/Keogh account	$		$
Employee retirement fund	$		$
Other	$		$
Consumption assets:			
Home furnishings/appliances	$	**Total liabilities**	$
Sports and hobby equipment	$		
Antiques, art, collections	$		
Jewelry, furs, etc.	$		
Automobiles/vehicles	$		
Other:			
	$	TOTAL ASSETS	$
	$	LESS TOTAL LIABILITIES	$
	$		
Total assets	$	NET WORTH	$

Worksheet 7 – Estimated Annual Income After Retirement

Enter all the sources of income you can count on and add up the amounts. Add up the estimates of income taxes you may have to pay and subtract them from your gross income to get an estimate of the net annual income you can expect in retirement.

Yearly Income

1. Social Security:
    Man's at age____
    Woman's at age____

2. Pensions and Employer Benefits:
    Company
    State or federal government
    Veteran's
    Union or other
    Profit sharing
    Deferred pay
    Other

3. Savings and Investments:
    IRA/Roth IRA
    Keogh or SEP
    Savings account (interest)
    Money market (interest)
    Treasury securities (interest)
    Mutual funds (dividends, capital gains)
    Stocks (dividends)
    Bonds (dividends)
    Real estate
    Farm/business rent or installment payments   _____
    Home equity conversion
    Annuities
    Other

4. Earnings:
    Salary, wages
    Commissions, royalties, fees
    Partnership income

5. Income from Assets That Could Be Liquidated
    Real estate
    Mutual funds
    Stocks
    Bonds
    Antiques, collectibles
    Farm/business
    Anticipated gifts or inheritance
    ESTIMATED TOTAL GROSS INCOME

6. Possible Deductions from Income
    Federal income tax
    State/county tax
    Social Security tax
    ESTIMATED TOTAL DEDUCTIONS

(Subtract total tax deductions from total gross income to estimate your total net income.)

TOTAL ESTIMATED NET INCOME

Retirement Planning

Worksheet 8 – Estimated Annual Income 10 Years After Retirement

Look 10 years into retirement and see how your estimated income will keep up with inflation. In the first column, copy your figures from Worksheet 7, "Estimated Annual Income After Retirement." Then, for each source of income, estimate how it will grow over the next 10 years. Some sources, like a pension or fixed annuity, will not change. For those sources that could change, use the same inflation rate from the table on page 7 that was used for completing Worksheet 4. Compare your estimated income 10 years after retirement with your estimated expenses 10 years after retirement.

Inflation Rate = _____ % (same as on Worksheet 4)

	Yearly Income at Retirement	Inflation Factor	Yearly Income 10 Years After Retirement
1. Social Security:			
Man's at age _____	_____	_____	_____
Woman's at age _____	_____	_____	_____
2. Pensions and Employer Benefits:			
Company	_____	_____	_____
State or federal government	_____	_____	_____
Veteran's	_____	_____	_____
Union or other	_____	_____	_____
Profit sharing	_____	_____	_____
Deferred pay	_____	_____	_____
Other	_____	_____	_____
3. Savings and Investments:			
IRA/Roth IRA	_____	_____	_____
Keogh or SEP	_____	_____	_____
Savings account (interest)	_____	_____	_____
Money market (interest)	_____	_____	_____
Treasury securities (interest)	_____	_____	_____
Mutual funds (dividends, capital gains)	_____	_____	_____
Stocks (dividends)	_____	_____	_____
Bonds (dividends)	_____	_____	_____
Real estate	_____	_____	_____
Farm/business rent or installment payments	_____	_____	_____
Home equity conversion	_____	_____	_____
Annuities	_____	_____	_____
Other	_____	_____	_____
4. Earnings:			
Salary, wages	_____	_____	_____
Commissions, royalties, fees	_____	_____	_____
Partnership income	_____	_____	_____

Worksheet 8 – *continued*

5. Income from Assets That Could Be Liquidated
   Real estate
   Mutual funds
   Stocks
   Bonds
   Antiques, collectibles
   Farm/business
   Anticipated gifts or inheritance

   ESTIMATED TOTAL GROSS INCOME

6. Possible Deductions from Income
   Federal income tax
   State/county tax
   Social Security tax
   ESTIMATED TOTAL DEDUCTIONS

(Subtract total tax deductions from total gross income to estimate your total net income.)

TOTAL ESTIMATED NET INCOME

Compare estimated income 10 years after retirement $ _____
to estimated expenses 10 years after retirement (Worksheet 4) (calculated
at inflation rate _____% with inflation factor of _____). $ _____

Will you have a positive balance of $_____ extra income?
                    OR
A negative balance of $_____ less income than expenses?

Retirement Planning

Worksheet 9 – Monthly Cost of Living Worksheet

Shelter		Medical and Health	
Rent or mortgage payments	$	Medications	$
Real estate taxes	$	Physician, dentist, hospital	$
Home insurance	$	Eyeglasses, hearing aids	$
		Health insurance	$
Household Operation and Maintenance		**Recreation, Education, and Other**	
Home repair, yard care	$	Books, newspapers, magazines	$
Water	$	Club memberships, dues	$
Telephone, TV dish/cable	$	Movies, sports events, concerts	$
Waste disposal	$	Sport and hobby equipment, supplies	$
Cleaning and laundry supplies	$	Vacations, celebrations, weekend trips	$
Electric	$	Adult continuing education	$
Gas, fuel oil	$	Pets: care, food, license	$
Furniture, fixtures	$	Other	$
Garden, yard equipment, supplies	$		
Other	$		
Food, Beverages		**Contributions**	
Food at home	$	Church	$
Food away from home	$	Charities	$
Entertaining expenses	$	Gifts	$
Automobile and Transportation		**Taxes and Insurance**	
Car payment	$	U.S. taxes	$
Repairs	$	State taxes	$
Gasoline and oil	$	Local taxes	$
License, registration	$	Life insurance	$
Insurance	$	Property insurance (not homeowners)	$
Other transportation	$		
Clothing		**Savings, Investments**	
New clothing	$	Banks, savings and loan, credit union	$
Laundry not done at home	$	Company pension, profit-sharing plan	$
Dry cleaning	$	Stocks, bonds, real estate	$
Shoe repair	$	Retirement: Keogh, IRA	$
Personal		**Irregular Expenses**	
Cosmetics and toiletries	$		$
Barber and beauty shops	$		$
Smoking supplies, alcohol	$		$
Stationery, postage	$		$
TOTAL MONTHLY EXPENSES			$

Please take your time and fill these 9 worksheets in the order they appear. You don't have to complete them in 1 day, 1 week, or even 1 month. Take your time so that you get everything right. This will go a very long way in helping you with your retirement plan.

Good luck!

About the Author

After a long and successful career in corporate America, I decided to write a book about retirement planning. I'm not a financial planner, but I have a lot of experience and knowledge about the topic. I want to share what I've learned with others who are nearing retirement age.

In my book, I talk about the different options for retirement, how to save money, and how to make the most of your retirement years. I also share my own personal story of retirement planning and offer advice to readers.

I hope that my book will help people to plan for their retirement in a way that works best for them. I also want to encourage people to enjoy their retirement years, and to make the most of them.

ANDREW J. BROWN

www.ingramcontent.com/pod-product-compliance
Lightning Source LLC
Chambersburg PA
CBHW020433220526
45464CB00002B/678